Jews and Saracens in the Consilia of Oldradus de Ponte

Norman Zacour

In the early decades of the fourteenth century Oldradus de Ponte, an advocate in the papal capital of Avignon, set about editing his *consilia* for publication. These were the hundreds of legal arguments he had made as a consultant during his career at the papal court. Their collection may not have been the first of its kind, but it was certainly among the earliest, and its size and scope ensured its wide circulation and influence.

In fact, it marked the beginning of a trend for the next three centuries, as succeeding generations of lawyers collected and circulated consilia to serve as professional manuals. Their immediacy and wealth of detail made them a refreshing change from the usually abstract discussions of the law. These very features now make them a rich source of material for the social history of the later Middle Ages.

Oldradus dealt with a greater variety of cases than many. His collection is unusual, for example, in its inclusion of several consilia on problems posed by the presence of communities of Jews and Muslims within Christian territories: enquiries about their expulsion, expropriation, taxation, conversion, and the like. These consilia, given here in translation as well as in their original Latin, are examined especially for the light they throw on the tendency in the west to disregard distinctions between Jews and Muslims and merge them into a single legal category.

STUDIES AND TEXTS 100

JEWS AND SARACENS IN THE CONSILIA OF OLDRADUS DE PONTE

NORMAN ZACOUR

PONTIFICAL INSTITUTE OF MEDIAEVAL STUDIES

ACKNOWLEDGMENTS

This book has been published with the help of a grant from the Social Science Federation of Canada, using funds provided by the Social Sciences and Humanities Research Council of Canada.

The illustration on the cover and on pages 1, 33, 71, and 91 is adapted from a manuscript of Gratian's *Decretum*, Causa 23, courtesy of the Walters Art Gallery, Baltimore (MS W.133, folio 213).

CANADIAN CATALOGUING IN PUBLICATION DATA

Zacour, Norman P.
Jews and Saracens in the consilia of Oldradus de Ponte

(Studies and texts, ISSN 0082-5328; 100)
Includes Latin texts with English translations.
Includes bibliographical references.
ISBN 0-88844-100-2

1. Jews - Legal status, laws, etc. - Europe - History. 2. Jews - Legal status, laws, etc. - Europe - History - Sources. 3. Muslims - Legal status, laws, etc. - Europe - History. 4. Muslims - Legal status, laws, etc. - Europe - History - Sources. 5. Oldrado da Ponte, d. 1335. I. Oldrado da Ponte, d. 1335. II. Pontifical Institute of Mediaeval Studies. III. Title. IV. Series: Studies and texts (Pontifical Institute of Mediaeval Studies); 100.

KJA2150.O53Z33 1990 340.5′5 C89-090753-6

Pontifical Institute of Mediaeval Studies
59 Queen's Park Crescent East
Toronto, Ontario, Canada M5S 2C4

PRINTED BY UNIVERSA, WETTEREN, BELGIUM

for

KENNETH M. SETTON
teacher and friend
on his 75th birthday

Contents

Preface

I began this study with two things in mind: to emphasize the importance of a neglected class of historical source, the *consilium*, a type of document that can throw much light on links between legal theory and legal practice in the later Middle Ages; and to examine certain such consilia touching on Jews and Muslims in Christian lands.

The consilia in question were written in the early decades of the fourteenth century by Oldradus de Ponte (d. 1337?), an advocate in the papal court of Avignon, and brought together in a collection of some 333 items. Of these, eight dealt with a variety of matters relevant to the study of Jews and Muslims in the West: the conversion of a Jew to Islam; enquiries of the Inquisitor of Crete about Jewish converts who had returned to Judaism; questions about the legitimacy of war against Saracens in Spain; the expulsion of Jews and Saracens; whether it was licit to use the help of 'infidels' in one's own defence; the trial in Avignon of a Jew who had had sexual relations with a Christian woman; whether Jews and Saracens should pay tithes to the Christian church, and so on.

Oldradus' collection of consilia is one of the earliest that we have. The many extant manuscript copies and printed editions of the work from the fourteenth century down to the seventeenth prove how popular and important it was. There remain thousands of consilia written by generations of jurists in the later Middle Ages that still lie unpublished, little known, waiting to be examined for the light they can shed on many aspects of the history of late-medieval society. My aim in what follows, therefore, has been a modest one: to bring the resources of one discipline to the assistance of another, to draw the attention of (in this case) students of the history of Jews and Muslims in western Europe to a handful of legal texts of a type not readily apprehended in the ordinary course of their studies, and to clarify these texts as much as possible. I can hardly claim that my own views of the subject are either exhaustive or conclusive. Others more directly involved in the study of Jewish or Muslim settlements in the medieval West will be able to place Oldradus under even greater obligation.

I have had the generous help of many. I must thank Joseph Goering and Joseph Shatzmiller of the University of Toronto, Giulio Silano of the Pontifical Institute of Mediaeval Studies, Jacqueline Brown of the Medieval Academy of America, James Brundage of The University of Kansas, and the readers of the Department of Publications at the Pontifical Institute of Mediaeval Studies for many corrections and helpful suggestions; and the Vatican Film Library of St. Louis University, the Kenneth Spencer Library of the University of Kansas, and the Library of the Institute for Advanced Study, Princeton, for the opportunity to examine copies of manuscripts and early printed editions of the consilia of Oldradus de Ponte. I alone am responsible, however, for whatever errors persist in the pages that follow.

Centre for Medieval Studies
University of Toronto
17 June 1989

INTRODUCTION

Introduction

Consilia

A medieval lawyer's consilium was usually his certified opinion about a case being heard or about to be heard by a court of law. The client for whom it was prepared might be a litigant but more often was the court itself, seeking help in settling a difficult case. The consilium took a certain form, naming the main parties to the case, reciting the facts, reviewing the relevant laws and their apparent contradictions, and bearing the name and the seal of the advocate (or advocates) who wrote it. Rarely, however, does it make for easy reading. It was heavily freighted with citations of canon law, Roman law, and the weightier commentators, and was embellished (almost compulsively so) by a style of legal scholarship that sought to strengthen every statement, no matter how trite, with the support of as many authorities as possible—a style of enduring popularity. In all fairness, however, it was assumed at the time that no one would read a consilium without a suitable library at hand. This would include the primary texts of civil and canon law and the major commentaries, at the very least the ordinary glosses.

The demand for and use of legal consilia grew very quickly after the end of the thirteenth century. From then until the seventeenth the practice of writing consilia spawned a large literature full of legal principles, precedents and model cases. It was a literature continually studied and cited,[1] in turn prompting successive generations of lawyers to publish yet more consilia. Most of these have reached us in the form of collections, in which we find each case introduced by the opinion of a principal advocate, often, though not always, followed by that of one or more colleagues supporting, adding to, or modifying the first, the whole

[1] The subtitle of one of the later editions of Oldradus de Ponte's consilia (1576) reads: "in quibus ea quae ad quotidianum usum in forensibus negotiis, et controversiis spectant, subtilissime et exactissime perstringuntur."

comprising a consilium.[2] Such collections served the purpose of case studies for judges and practicing advocates.

Increasingly in the Middle Ages law courts in Spain, Italy, southern Germany and Mediterranean France were confronted with a multitude of local codes, customs and jurisdictions, and often had to rely on the advice of local experts to avoid confusion. James I of Aragon had put his finger on the problem as early as the middle of the thirteenth century: "In any king's court there should be canonists, civilians, and experts in customary law with him, for all kinds of pleas come before him. By the mercy of God for which I give thanks, I have three or four kingdoms where many kinds of cases come up. If I did not have people with whom to deliberate, it would shame me and my court, for neither we nor any non-professional can be learned in the law books everywhere. ... That is why I have these men with me."[3] The "assessor," as the professional legal consultant might be called, was an important adjunct of the court. In later years collections of the consilia of such consultants, in effect the case studies of legal experts, would come to be of great practical importance to the judicial system especially of southern Europe. Later still, when for various reasons the need for them declined, such collections fell into disuse and were soon forgotten. Until recently they have been all but ignored. This is understandable enough but a pity just the same, for they throw light on the links between legal theory and practice in the later Middle Ages. At a less exalted level they sometimes preserve odd, long-forgotten historical facts.[4]

[2] For a good example, see Mario Ascheri, "Analecta manoscritta consiliare (1285–1354)," *Bulletin of Medieval Canon Law*, new series, 15 (1985) 61–94, especially the photograph (facing p. 66) of the seals of 13 consultants on a single consilium of 1327. And see below, p. 10, notes 32, 33. The word consilium might be used to describe either the totality of opinions of all the consultants in a case or the particular argument of any one of them, although in the latter case the more usual term, to judge from the collection of Oldradus de Ponte, was *allegationes*.

[3] R.I. Burns, *Muslims, Christians and Jews in the Crusader Kingdom of Valencia* (Cambridge, 1984), p. 253.

[4] On the importance and influence of the consilium, see Norbert Horn, "Die legistische Literatur der Kommentatoren und der Ausbreitung des gelehrten Rechts," in *Handbuch der Quellen und Literatur der neueren europäischen Privatrechtsgeschichte*, I, *Mittelalter (1100–1500): Die gelehrten Rechte und die Gesetzgebung*, ed. Helmut Coing (Munich, 1973), p. 336: "... nach seinen wissenschaftlichen Qualität und wegen seiner Bedeutung für die Rechtspraxis ist das Consilium eine der wichtigsten, vielleicht die wichtigste Literaturform der Epoche"; and Ingrid Baumgärtner, "Consilia–Quellen zur Familie in Krise und Kontinuität," in *Die Familie als sozialer und historischer Verband*, ed. Peter-Johannes Schuler (Sigmaringen, 1987), p. 43: "In der historischen Forschung fanden diese *consilia* gemessen an ihrem Quellenwert bislang viel zu wenig Beachtung, obgleich sie oft reichhaltige und singuläre Auskünfte zu Personen, Lebensgemeinschaften, Institutionen und die damit

The fact that consilia were also called other things—*responsa*, *allegationes*, *quaestiones*[5]—reminds us that they sometimes had nothing to do with court cases. Then as now administrators needed the kind of sensible advice that lawyers claim to specialize in, namely, how to manage affairs while staying within the law. It was a need that made large demands on the advocate's talents. At all levels of government—of state, church, or community—officials sought legal advice in matters of finance, administration, politics, justice. The traditional consilium turned out to be an ideal instrument for the purpose. As a result, many of these neglected texts take on historical interest. For example, there is the consilium of two Venetian jurisconsults who were asked by the Doge to examine the claims of an Inquisitor who wanted to punish Jews for alleged blasphemy of the cross.[6] Indeed, as a form of consultation the consilium proved to be ideal for political as well as strictly legal purposes. A case in point is the large consilium comprising the opinions of some seventeen cardinals preserved in a register of the correspondence of Pope John XXII. The cardinals advised the pope on the question of the nature and extent of the help that they thought he should or should not give the king of France for a prospective crusade. Their consilium is a mine of information about the give and take of diplomacy in the fourteenth century.[7]

In fact, one of the most demanding clients, often beset with legal problems, was precisely the apostolic see in Avignon. Popes had long observed the proverb "Ubi multa consilia, ibi salus."[8] Not surprisingly, papal Avignon gave birth to one of the earliest and most important collections of consilia. It rehearses cases and questions that had arisen, for the most part, during the 1320s. It is not, however, a composite collection of the type described above, i.e. the opinions of several counsellors, but

verbundenen privaten und politischen Ereignisse liefern und zudem Einblick in grundlegende wirtschaftliche und soziale Verhältnisse ermöglichen." See also Peter Riesenberg, "The Consilia Literature: A Prospectus," *Manuscripta* 6 (1962) 3–22; Guido Kisch, *Consilia: Eine Bibliographie der juristischen Konsiliensammlungen* (Basel, 1970).

[5] Cf. Vatican City, Biblioteca Vaticana, Ross. 1096, f. 195: "Incipit tabula questionum consiliorum et allegacionum domini Oldradi de Laude."

[6] David Jacoby, "Venice, the Inquisition and the Jewish Communities of Crete in the Early 14th Century," *Studi veneziani* [Florence] 12 (1970) 127–144; rpt. in David Jacoby, *Recherches sur la Méditerranée orientale du XIIe au XVe siècle: peuples, sociétés, économies*, Variorum Reprints (London, 1979), with a letter of the Venetian Doge in 1314 summarizing the consilium.

[7] Auguste Coulon and S. Clémencet, *Lettres secrètes et curiales du pape Jean XXII relatives à la France* (Paris, 1913–1972), 2:281–318, nos. 1692–1709.

[8] Prov 11:14, a favourite text of Innocent III (PL 215:1128).

rather the collection of a single advocate of growing reputation at the time, one Oldradus de Ponte.

Oldradus

He came from Lodi, near Milan. De Ponte was his family name. We have only a few meagre facts about his career, strung together from passing comments made by two or three acquaintances including the canonist Johannes Andreae and the poet Petrarch. Petrarch, very much his junior, knew him in Avignon, possibly through their mutual connections with the powerful Colonna family of Rome, and called him the most illustrious jurist of the age.[9] Oldradus studied law at the university of Bologna with Dinus de Mugello who taught there from 1284 to 1297, and with Jacobus de Arena, who taught there between 1287 and 1296. He had entered the service of cardinal Peter Colonna by 1297[10]—not a good year, for in May, 1297, Pope Boniface VIII deposed the two Colonna cardinals, Peter and his uncle James, incidentally nipping in the bud Oldradus' career as a curialist. He was then employed as Assessor by Fissirago Bresciano, Capitano del Popolo of Bologna. Later, he taught law at the university of Padua. The canonist Johannes Andreae knew him there, and mentions his legal discussions and disputations.[11]

From Padua, where he taught until a little after 1310,[12] he went to Avignon. There he spent the rest of his life. Clement V had reinstated the Colonna cardinals in December, 1305, and service with his old patron probably drew Oldradus to the court. There is some reason to think that he may have entered or re-entered the household of the cardinal as a 'familiar': Cardinal Peter recommended that Oldradus' son John be provided with a canonry and expectation of a prebend in the church of

[9] *Epistolae familiares* 4.16, in Vittorio Rossi (ed.), *Francesco Petrarca: Familiari, edizione critica*, Edizione nazionale delle opere di Francesco Petrarca 10 (Florence, 1968) 1:196.

[10] Pierre Dupuy, *Histoire du differend d'entre le pape Boniface VIII. et Philippes le bel roy de France* (1655; rpt. Tucson, 1963), p. 33.

[11] Cf. Eduard Will, *Die Gutachten des Oldradus de Ponte zum Prozess Heinrichs VII. gegen Robert von Neapel, nebst der Biographie des Oldradus* (Abhandlungen zur mittleren und neueren Geschichte 65, Berlin and Leipzig, 1917), pp. 1–5.

[12] G. Panzirolo, *De claris legum interpretatibus libri quattuor* (Padua, 1565): "Ego ipsum paulo post annum 1310 Patavi docentem in eius urbis iurisconsultorum albo scriptum legi," cited by Will, p. 8, note 23.

Padua (1316),[13] the sort of thing that cardinals were expected to do for their familiars.[14]

His Career in Avignon

Oldradus would describe himself as "legum professor et advocatus in Romana curia."[15] He may have taught law in the papal *studium* in Avignon, but it is more likely that the title of professor refers merely to his having once taught at Padua. There is evidence also that if he was not formally an auditor of the Rota he was closely associated with those who were, participating in their discussions. Thomas Fastolf, in his short diary of cases and conferences in the Rota in 1336–1337, mentions a certain "Oldr." discussing a case with the auditors, for the identity of whom the only candidate we have is Oldradus de Ponte.[16]

[13] Guillaume Mollat, *Jean XXII (1316–1334): Lettres communes*, 16 vols. (Paris, 1904–1947), 1:128 (no. 1325). For other papal concessions to his children, see Arnold Fayen, *Lettres de Jean XXII*, Analecta vaticano-belgica, vols. 2 and 3 (Paris and Rome, 1908), 1:325 (no. 801), 479 (no. 1293), 533 (no. 1436); 2:384 (no. 2698), 661 (no. 3417); Alphonse Fierens, *Lettres de Benoît XII*, Analecta vaticano-belgica, vol. 4 (Paris and Rome, 1910), p. 422 (nos. 879, 881); cf. Mollat, 3:70 (no. 11063); 5:241 (no. 20845); 8:299 (no. 45510); 9:273 (no. 49168); J.M. Vidal, *Benoît XII (1334–1342): Lettres communes* 3 vols. (Paris, 1903–1911), 1:65 (no. 585). He had three sons, John, who followed in his footsteps as lawyer, scholar and teacher, James and Peter.

[14] See Norman Zacour, "Papal Regulation of Cardinals' Households in the Fourteenth Century," *Speculum* 50 (1975) 434–455; *idem*, "Petrus de Braco and His *Repudium Ambitionis*," *Mediaeval Studies* 41 (1979) 1–29.

[15] Cons. 289: "Mihi Oldrado de ponte de laude legum professori et advocato in Romana curia ad praedictas allegationes videtur addendum quod sequitur, videlicet... ." In the various papal grants made to his sons, Oldradus is usually mentioned as "legum doctor" or (in 1335) "magister et legum doctor" (Vidal, *Benoît XII*, 1:65 [no. 585]).

[16] *Dominorum de Rota decisiones novae, antiquae et antiquiores* (Lyons, 1562), where he is mentioned twice, p. 652 (causa 31, dubia 60; causa 32, dubia 61). If this was Oldradus, and there is no evidence that it could have been anyone else, it indicates that he was alive in February 1337 and that the date usually given for his death, 1335, is wrong. The evidence for that date has been a nearly illegible inscription which in part was read as: "Qui obiit anno 1335 die Lunae Idus mensis Aprilis sexto"; since 8 April 1335 did not fall on a Monday, we may assume that either the inscription was mistaken or that it was misinterpreted (cf. Will, *Gutachten*, p. 16). Another reading which fixed the date as 13 April, still not a Monday, may be found in Luigi Anfosso, "Oldrado da Ponte e le sue opere," *Archivio storico per la città e communi del circondario di Lodi* 32 (1913) 101–116 (see p. 104), a work which is also unreliable in most other respects.

Fastolf's *Decisiones* should be compared with the 13 consilia from precisely the same period, December 1336 to February 1337, written by some of the same auditors of the Rota whom he himself often names; see Marita Kremer, *Manuscripta Iuridica*, Die Handschriften der murhardschen Bibliothek der Stadt Kassel und Landesbibliothek 2 (Wiesbaden, 1969), ms.iurid. 23, ff. 271–281v.

While we know nothing of his personal life, we can be sure that the range of his influence in the circle of papal counsellors was considerable, to judge from the nature and importance of the many questions on which he would be consulted.[17] We no longer have his commentaries, but we know that he annotated civil law texts.[18] As a legal counsellor he was as much concerned with important feudal cases[19] as with the rights of ecclesiastics.[20] He was called upon more than once to defend the brothers of St. Anthony who ran the hospital in Avignon for the papal court. The dispute was a chronic one having to do with the burial fees of curialists, especially of cardinals who were trying to avoid the expense.[21] Pope John XXII often asked Oldradus for his opinion in delicate matters of importance, such as the dismissal of Foulque de Villaret, the Grand Master of the convent of the Hospital of St. John of Jerusalem,[22] and consulted him among others on questions relating to the double election in Germany.[23]

On Thomas Fastolf, see Gero Dolezalek, "Quaestiones motae in Rota: Richterliche Beratungsnotizien aus dem vierzehnten Jahrhundert," *Proceedings of the Fifth International Congress of Medieval Canon Law, Salamanca, 21–25 September 1976*, ed. by Stephan Kuttner and Kenneth Pennington (Città del Vaticano, 1980), pp. 99–114, esp. pp. 102–104.

[17] For the influence of his Cons. 43 on the formation of the papal bull *Pastoralis cura*, see Eduard Will, *Die Gutachten des Oldradus de Ponte*, pp. 20–51.

[18] An inventory of the books of Johannes de Capua, LL.D., drawn up in Sicily in 1475, contained a "Librum Lecture Domini Oldradi in carta bonbicina"; see Henri Bresc, *Livre et société en Sicile (1299–1499)* (Palermo, 1971), p. 254, no. 166 (8). See also *Codices Urbinates Latini*, ed. C. Stornajolo (Rome, 1902), 1:170 (no. 166); *Codici miniati dell'Ambrosiana: Contributo a un catalogo*, ed. Renata Cipriani (Milan, 1968), p. 228 (no. D534 inf.); and *Die Handschriften des Bartholomaeusstifts und des Karmeliterklosters in Frankfurt am Main*, ed. Gerhardt Powitz and Herbert Buck, Kataloge der Stadt- und Universitätsbibliothek Frankfurt am Main, ed. C. Köttelnesch, vol. 3 (Frankfurt, 1974), pp. 23, 35. For some of Oldradus' glosses on the *libri feudorum* see Biblioteca Vaticana, Reg. lat. 1063, ff. 300v, 308v, 309, 315r, cited in G. Giordanengo, "Note sur un manuscrit juridique du Midi de la France (*Vat.Lat.* 2642)," *Revue historique de droit français et étranger* 49 (1971) 100.

[19] Cons. 224, a case respecting rights of primogeniture in the county of S. Severin, heard in Avignon before Robert, king of Sicily, and the cardinals Bertrand de Montfavès and Giovanni Gaetani Orsini.

[20] Cons. 239, dealing with the role of the Archbishop of Toulouse as conservator of the rights of Raymond de Fargues, who had been made a cardinal by Clement V in 1310. He died 5 October 1346; cf. Etienne Baluze, *Vitae paparum Avenionensium*, ed. Guillaume Mollat, 4 vols. (Paris, 1914–1927), 2:147–149.

[21] Cons. 211, 293, 321.

[22] Cons. 128: "... because of certain illicit excesses, waste, and great offences which, from reverence for Your Holiness and the Holy See ... I pass over in silence since they are thought to be widely known, and because I understand that Your Holiness has been informed by certain special investigators whom you recently sent to Rhodes ... ."

[23] Cons. 22 and 23.

Clearly, then, not all his consilia were about cases before the courts. Some reflect debates in Avignon which allow a brief, tantalizing glimpse of some of the intellectual and political concerns of the time, often interesting, occasionally trivial. For example, there was the question of whether a person could have too many books, which he quickly swept aside with the help, among others, of Thomas Aquinas who, it was said, would rather own a copy of Chrysostom's commentary on Matthew than the city of Paris.[24] In another consilium, addressed directly to Pope John XXII, Oldradus urged the return of the papal curia to Rome. It reflects his personal participation in what must have been a vigorous debate in Avignon after the papal legate in Italy, cardinal Bertrand de Poujet, took Bologna in 1327 and so briefly opened the way for the papacy to move to Italy.[25] As one of a band of Italian expatriates in Avignon, Oldradus hoped that Pope John XXII would soon move the court to what every Italian knew in his heart was its natural home. Yet another finds him pleading for moderation in the treatment of someone associated with "infideles et rebelles ecclesie"—some leader "qui ultra omnes deliquit et fuit caput scandali et petra offensionis";[26] if the pope were to show clemency towards him, his followers might be more inclined to return to obedience. In the 1320s there were a lot of Franciscans shuffling in and out of the papal prison in Avignon. To judge from the importance of this unnamed offender, it is possible that Oldradus here is expressing some cautious sympathy for the deposed general of the Franciscan order, Michael of Cesena, in 1328.[27] His consilium on a matter concerning the emperor Henry VII and King Robert of Naples has proved to be an invaluable source;[28] and another has been used to illustrate his teaching at the University of Padua.[29]

On the whole, then, we have a picture of an advocate and legal authority of some distinction, well regarded by his colleagues, in regular contact with major figures in the papal court, frequently consulted in matters of importance, and whose many consultations, therefore, are now of substantial historical interest.

[24] Cons. 84: "Et narratur quod beatus Thomas dixit, quod magis vellet habere Chrysostomum super Matthaeum quam civitatem Parisius."

[25] Cons. 85.

[26] Isaiah 8:14; cf. 1 Peter 2:8.

[27] Cons. 47. The question of fugitive Franciscans is also the subject of Cons. 65.

[28] See Eduard Will, *Die Gutachten des Oldradus de Ponte* cited above, note 11.

[29] See Francesco Migliorino, "Alchimia lecita e illecita nel Trecento: Oldrado da Ponte," *Quaderni medievali* 11 (1981) 6–41.

The Collection

Unfortunately, what we do not have is an adequate edition of his consilia. The work went through several editions in the fifteenth and sixteenth centuries, and then dropped from sight.[30] Its core seems to have been an original collection, probably prepared by Oldradus himself, of 264 items, to which later editors would append other consilia that were "extravagantes," so to speak, scattered among miscellaneous collections of consilia to be found in Avignon.[31] One manuscript mentions an addition of some ten items to the original collection, drawn from works containing the joint consilia of several authors, bringing the total to 274.[32] Later printed editions, enlarged yet further, preserve references to two additional accretions of some significance: 26 items found in a single volume, a miscellaneous collection;[33] and then another 43, many of them bearing Oldradus' name, again culled from some miscellany of consilia in Avignon written by various lawyers.[34] This brought the total to 333.[35]

[30] See below, Appendix.

[31] For an example, including some contributions by Oldradus, see Giordanengo, "Note sur un manuscrit juridique du Midi de la France (*Vat.Lat.* 2642)," pp. 95–107.

[32] Vatican City, Biblioteca Vaticana, MS Ross.1096, f. 174 (following Cons. 264): "Communiter hic finiuntur consilia oldradi, sed aliqui libri habent consilia que sequuntur, quorum quedam sunt diversorum doctorum prout in aliquibus eorum per expressionem propriorum nominum evidenter apparet." Oldradus did not write Cons. 266, 271–273.

[33] See *Oldradi de Ponte Laudensis ... Consilia, seu Responsa* (Frankfurt, 1576), f. 161: "Haec quae sequuntur consilia in uno duntaxat ac singulari codice sunt inventa, quae etsi longa iam vetustate multis sint ignota, ea tamen sunt eiusmodi, ut omnium consensu, qui de hac re iudicare possent, Oldradi esse non dubitentur." The editing was not always very carefully done; Cons. 276 repeats Cons. 239. See f. 169v for the company that Cons. 289 kept: "Not. quod hoc consilium fuit subscriptio ad consilium Domini Fed. de Sen. 154, cui pariter consilia subscripserunt D. Petrus de Ferro, D. Raynerius Abbas de Pudio Boni, D. Bernardus de Montesio, et D. Pacificus de Plano."

[34] Ibid, f. 170: "Haec quae sequuntur consilia et quod proximo loco ante ponitur Avinioni sunt reperta, tanto plus gratiae secum afferentia quanto longius a consuetudine nostra demigrarunt."

[35] The order of the consilia, therefore, bore no relation to the standard organization of canon law established by Gregory IX's *Decretals*. Later editors, however, tried to associate the consilia with the various titles of the *Decretals*. For example, in MS Ross. 1096 (f. 195) an index to the consilia is organized by such titles as *De constitutionibus*, *De consuetudine*, *De electione*, etc., followed at the end by a catch-all "Extraordinaria." Kues MS 277, on the other hand, has its 273 consilia divided into two parts, depending on whether each is related more closely to civil or to canon law; the two parts are titled: "Allegationes centum in iure civili" (ff. 1–48); and "Questiones 173 in iure canonico" (ff. 48–151). See Jakob Marx, *Verzeichnis der Handschriften-Sammlung des Hospitals zu Cues* (1905; rpt. Frankfurt, 1966), p. 268 (no. 277).

Presumably Oldradus himself, or someone close to him either in his lifetime or shortly thereafter, prepared the original collection, the first 264 consilia. These show evidence of much editing. The formulas usually to be found in untouched consilia are missing.[36] Only a few reveal the identity of the parties involved. All of this suggests that we have here something more than an archive of discrete legal opinions. In fact, it has all the earmarks of a self-conscious contribution to legal scholarship, not so much along the lines of traditional commentaries, perhaps, but still reflecting the author's experience as a lawyer and a consultant, using material drawn from actual cases.[37] On the other hand, many of the later additions to the collection, neither edited nor integrated into the collection with the same care, retain Oldradus' name and abbreviated closing formulas, evidence of their more primitive form.[38]

While many of Oldradus' consilia clearly refer to some contemporary matter or other, mostly of the 1320s, it is often difficult to relate them to known events. Some are in the form of hypothetical cases, at one time probably real enough but now discussed in an abstract style reminiscent of the law that Oldradus studied in Bologna, a law seeking to establish principles of general application. The protagonist in such cases was often the darling of Roman jurists, Titius: "Titius dedit duobus coniugibus matrimonialiter iunctis omnia bona sua ..." and then wants to cancel the gift later. What are the rights in the matter? Or "Titius habens unam filiam ..." etc.[39]

Here, however, we are interested in those few consilia that Oldradus wrote on questions having to do with Jews, Muslims, or both. Again, the

[36] See Ascheri, "Analecta manoscritta consiliare (1285–1354)," pp. 61–94, for diplomatic examples of consilia, with opening formulae, the names of the parties involved, the names of the lawyers consulted, the dates of the consilia, notarial authentication, the subscriptions of colleagues indicating collaborative production, and even, in one case (p. 80), a record of payment for a consilium—eight gold florins.

[37] For an illustration of the transformation into abstract models of working consilia of particular cases, see Giuseppina Nicolosi Grassi, "Analisi di manoscritti vaticani per uno studio dei 'Consilia' di Giovanni e Gaspare Calderini," *Rivista di storia del diritto italiano* 50 (1977) 127–212, esp. 151 ff.

[38] "Cetera paternitatis vestre suppleat plenitudo, etc. Oldradus" (304); "Cetera suppleat equitas iudicantis. Oldradus" (313); "Atque hec brevitatis causa sufficiant. Cetera suppleat exuberans cognitio ius dicentis. Oldradus" (314); "Cetera suppleat religio iudicantis, et hec Oldradus" (315); "Cetera suppleat religio iudicantis. Et hoc est verum. Oldradus" (316); "Cetera suppleat equitas iudicantis. Et hec est verum. Oldradus" (318); "Hec sufficiant canoniste et theologo grosso; gentibus vobis subtilia argumenta legalia adiungetis" (264); "Ego Oldradus predicta scripsi et sigillum apposui" (333). For manuscripts and editions of the collection, see below, Appendix.

[39] Cons. 16, 108, 116, 119, 160, 171, 175, etc.

particular occasions that gave rise to most of these consilia, like so many others, is unknown. There were only eight of them. They were written in response to specific questions; as far as their origins are concerned, they have no integrity as a group. In other words, they reflect no attempt at a comprehensive discussion of non-Christian peoples. Nothing could have been further from their author's mind.[40] They do achieve a certain coherence, however, from his steady application to Jews and Muslims of standard texts drawn from both Roman civil law and canon law.[41] Moreover, unlike commonplace tracts attacking Jews or Muslims, or laws limiting contacts between Christians and 'infidels,' they provide, though in limited fashion, concrete examples of how, and the extent to which, canon and Roman civil law might be used to constrain Jews and Muslims, how popular notions of 'outsiders' were given a legal basis, and how attitudes towards different groups could reinforce one another. We can be grateful to Oldradus, then, not for some treatise on religious minorities, which never entered his mind, nor indeed (since his was a profession that held novelty suspect) for any original thought on the subject at all, but for a demonstration of how legal principles, developed in academic circles, could be applied to real cases of broad social and political significance.

Jews

To read only the opening sentences of these consilia is to be reminded of the growing concern among medieval churchmen about Judaism—the social mingling of Jews and Christians, the pervasive harmony of communities where Jews and Christians lived as neighbours, the distressing prospects of intermarriage, Jewish adoption of Christian children, the problems posed by relapsed converts, and so on. Christian authorities made a strong effort from the thirteenth century on to keep Christian and Jew apart. Of the many instruments at hand, one of the more important was the canon of the Fourth Lateran Council ordering that Jews and Muslims wear distinguishing garments the better to prevent any mingling

[40] To overlook this, to say only that he "concentrated his attention on the status of infidels who were living in Europe," and "focussed on the problem of infidels living in Spain" (James Muldoon, *Popes, Lawyers, and Infidels* [Liverpool, 1979], p.19; cf. p.25), all of which is true enough, can be misleading, for it suggests that the subjects of these consilia were of Oldradus' own choosing. In fact, authors of consilia concentrated their attention and focussed on problems put to them by others.

[41] See Walter Pakter, *De his qui foris sunt: The Teachings of the Medieval Canon and Civil Lawyers concerning the Jews* (Doctoral diss., Johns Hopkins University, 1974), pp. 1–39.

of the sexes across religious bounds.[42] Another was the insistence on separate quarters for Jews (and Saracens too, in Spain) especially in those places where they were numerous.[43] Other legal elements were equally useful. In his responses especially to the questions raised by the inquisitor of Crete, Andreas Doto (in Cons. 36 below), Oldradus sought to strengthen the notion of separation by harping on the old idea of the 'servitude' of the Jews. By so doing, by likening Jews to serfs or slaves, he could confirm principles for dealing with Jews by pressing into service Roman Law texts which dealt not with Jews but with the slaves of ancient Rome—texts which would hardly have suggested themselves otherwise, but which now took on new life.[44]

Churchmen might also exert authority over Jews by defining certain offences as 'ecclesiastical.' For example, the Aragonese inquisitor Johannes de Lotgerio, in a well known letter to James II of Aragon in 1302, claimed jurisdiction in the case of some Jews who were alleged to have insulted the Christian religion by spitting on a picture of the Virgin in a church in Alexandria: "et cum ... crimen esset ecclesiasticum ... super predictis inquisivimus diligenter."[45] In a similar case, as will be seen, Oldradus refused the inquisitor of Crete the same kind of freedom, but on the other hand he was expressly solicitous of his rights in the case of relapsed Jewish converts. He called them traitors, their defenders "prevaricatores" and "calumniatores," categories recognized and provided for by Roman Law.

[42] X, 5.6.15: "Contingit ... quod per errorem Christiani Judaeorum seu Saracenorum, et Judei seu Saraceni Christianorum mulieribus commiscentur." On the other hand, personal relationships between Jews and Muslims were not a matter for the church to meddle with, and were usually handled locally by the communities concerned. Cons. 51 below is therefore exceptional.

[43] Archivio Segreto Vaticano, Reg. Vat. 135, f. 1, Benedict XII to King Peter of Aragon, 8 January 1340: "... olim Iudeis et Sarracenis, in nonnullis civitatibus, castris et locis...in magna multitudine morantibus, certa loca clausa et distincta parietibus ad inhabitandum et negociandum, ut essent a familiaritate et conversatione Christianorum fidelium nimia periculosa remoti, ab antiquo fuerint deputata... ." Cf. Caesar Baronius, *Annales ecclesiastici*, 37 vols. (Bar-le-Duc, 1864–1888), an. 1340, §56–57.

[44] Below, pp. 38, 40, notes 6, 7, 23. Cf. Salo Wittmayer Baron, "Plenitude of Apostolic Powers and Medieval Jewish Serfdom," in *Ancient and Medieval Jewish History*, ed. Leon A. Feldman (New Brunswick, N.J., 1972), pp. 286–307. For Saracens as royal property in Spain, see Burns, *Muslims, Christians and Jews*, p. 250. Oldradus probably wrote Cons. 36 in 1326 when Andreas Doto was in Avignon; see R. Loenertz, "Documents pour servir à l'histoire de la province dominicaine de Grèce (1474–1669)," *Archivum fratrum praedicatorum* 14 (1944) p. 74, note 2; discussed by Jacoby, cited above, note 6.

[45] Heinrich Finke, *Acta Aragonensia: Quellen zur deutschen, italienischen, französischen, spanischen, zur Kirchen- und Kulturgeschichte aus der diplomatischen Korrespondenz Jaymes I. (1291–1327)*, 3 vols. (Berlin and Leipzig, 1908), 2:111–112 (no. 49).

Depending on the nature of the offence, then, Jews could be subject to prosecution in a church court—in effect, the inquisitional court.[46]

Most important, however, was the papal claim, asserted by Pope Innocent IV and reasserted by subsequent canonists, to jurisdiction over Jews where they transgressed their own law, the Mosaic law, and their leaders failed to punish them. Thus Innocent justified the steps that he and his predecessor, Gregory IX, took to destroy the Talmud, the reason being that the Talmud contained deviations from the moral law of the Old Testament as understood by the Church.[47]

The law also offered weapons with which to attack another worrisome problem echoed in these consilia, the tendency for converts from Judaism, secretly attached to their earlier faith, to revert to it when it was safe to do so. To put it bluntly, conversions to Christianity were rarely wholehearted, a fact not lost on contemporaries. Churchmen deplored compulsory conversion—indeed, condemned it—but it was rare indeed for them to admit after the fact that any particular such conversion was invalid.[48] We may be tempted to see as somewhat conventional, therefore, the citation in Oldradus' work, as in that of many others, of the canonical text that Jews were to be won to Christianity with kindness, presumably to ensure more willing conversions and to forestall later relapses. The unhappy fact was that the circumstances of most conversions were rarely so ideal, and once one had become a Christian, whatever the circumstances, one's return to Judaism was considered an act of heresy, the deserter and his supporters heretics. Oldradus bolstered this with principles derived from Roman law, like that which held that the harbourer of a brigand was to be treated as a brigand, thus confirming that inquisitors could treat as a heretic a Jewish harbourer of a relapsed convert. For that matter, the Roman law of late antiquity confirmed that anyone who persuaded a slave to abandon Christianity was to suffer capital punishment.[49] To Oldradus, for whom slave was a metaphor for Jew, the matter seemed clear enough.

Moreover, the convert must always have been suspect, never fully accepted. The development of a class of new Christians to mark them off

[46] See below, Cons. 36. It was on this very point that Oldradus would be cited as an authority in fifteenth-century Florence; Biblioteca Vaticana, Urb. Lat. 1132, f. 364r: "Et ita loquitur Oldradus suo consilio xxxv [sic]."

[47] Benjamin Z. Kedar, "Canon Law and the Burning of the Talmud," *Bulletin of Medieval Canon Law* 9 (1979) 79–82.

[48] Cf. Solomon Grayzel, "The Papal Bull *Sicut judeis*," *Studies and Essays in Honor of Abraham A. Neuman* (Leiden, 1962), pp. 278–279; and below, Cons. 51, 72.

[49] Below, Cons. 36.

from old Christians, which finds an echo in one of these consilia, tells us as much.[50] And at a more vulgar level old attitudes changed not at all. Frederick III of Trinacria (Sicily) published a constitution on Jews and Muslims in 1310, among much else reprimanding slave owners who prevented the conversion of their Muslim slaves to Christianity. Conceding that slaves need not be manumitted through baptism, fear of which was the reason for the opposition, he still insisted that they be treated humanely and no longer called "renegade dogs" according to the local custom of always calling Jews and Muslims dogs. There were some stigmata that conversion to Christianity could not remove.[51]

The consilia of Oldradus also reflect, however, the fundamental teaching, from the time of St. Augustine on,[52] respecting the relationship of Christians and Jews. This was based on the role of the Jew as witness to the Christian faith, to be enlightened finally by Christ at the end of the world. Since Paul had taught that the remnant of Israel would be saved at the end of time, Jews had, therefore, to be tolerated and protected in order to fulfil the law. The fact that this may have been a hackneyed teaching, that it was often widely flouted, or that the toleration it bespoke was usually thought of as an act of grace to be made or withheld as the occasion dictated, did not detract from its persistent force far into the future. It would continue to serve well beyond the Middle Ages as the foundation of a papal policy that sought to protect the Jews of Europe as necessary witnesses of Christ, and therefore to shelter them from unjust persecution,

[50] See Cons. 51 below. The distinction between the 'full,' or born Christian, and the convert, especially the Jewish convert, had a long history. During the vexed controversy over the papal election of 1130, for example, a supporter of Innocent II would dismiss Innocent's rival, Anacletus II, for being a (fourth generation) descendent of a Jewish convert, and so a member of a family still far from being cleansed of the yeast of Jewish corruption; "... familia ... nondum fermento iudaicae corruptionis penitus expiata"; see Johann Matthias Watterich, *Pontificum Romanorum qui fuerunt inde ab exeunte saeculo IX usque ad finem saeculi XIII vitae* ..., 2 vols. (1862; rpt. Aalen, 1966) 2:274. Likewise, Bernard of Clairvaux could not stomach the thought of a descendent of a Jew on the papal throne; it would be an insult to Christ. See his letter no. 139 to the emperor Lothar in 1134, in *Sancti Bernardi Opera*, ed. Jean Leclercq and H. Rochais (Rome, 1974) 3:335–336.

[51] Heinrich Finke, *Acta Aragonensia* 2:695–699; cf. Benjamin Z. Kedar, *Crusade and Mission: European Approaches toward the Muslims* (Princeton, 1984), pp. 146–150; Dolors Bramon, *Contra Moros i Jueus: Formació i estratègia d'unes discriminacions al país Valencià* (Valencia, 1981), p. 66: "La documentació coetània assenyala escrupolosament la seva condició de cristians nous, de *çaenrere* jueus, de novellament convertits o de neòfits, tot apareixent, com a conseqüència, la diferenciació de cristià vell i de cristià de natura. Dintre del mateix ordre de coses és ben significatiu el privilegi de Jaume II de 1297 que prohibia anomenar-los 'renegat vel tornadiç vel alio verbo'... ."

[52] See, for example, Cons. 87 below.

prevent their elimination from Christian lands, and keep them safe until the end of time—provided, of course, that they accept their servile status. They might persist in their stubborn refusal to recognize Christ now, but they would come to see the truth in time, drawn to it by the customary grace of the pope's protection.[53]

Saracens

One might think that in the medieval West the distinction between Jews and Muslims must have been clear. Yet it was often not necessary to treat them separately.[54] What for Oldradus marked them off one from the other was not, as we might think, differences of religion, but rather their relationship to Christendom. The distinction was succinctly defined in the eleventh century by Pope Alexander II, a brief portion of whose letter Gratian would include in his *Decretum* under a heading that said all that there was to be said: "Iudeos non debemus persequi, sed Sarracenos." "There is a marked difference," Alexander wrote, "between the cases of Jews and Saracens. Against the latter, who persecute Christians, who drive them from their towns and their dwellings, warfare is justified; the former are everywhere prepared to serve."[55]

[53] The exordia of papal letters responding to petitions from Jews continually rehearse such themes. For an example from the fifteenth century, see the letter of Eugenius IV, 18 November 1439, in August Theiner, *Codex diplomaticus dominii temporalis s. sedis*, 3 vols. (1862; rpt. Frankfurt, 1964), 3:342 (no. 290): "Quamvis Judei, quos in testimonium Ihesu Christi sacrosancta diversis locis ecclesia tollerat, in eorum potius duritia cecitateque persistere velint, quam prophetarum verba et sacrarum archana scripturarum cognoscere, ad Christiane quoque fidei et salutis noticiam pervenire: quia tamen in eorum necessitatibus nostra presidia et favores interpellant, nos ipsis Christiane pietatis mansuetudinem et clemenciam denegare non intendimus, ut sic allecti suos cognoscere curent errores, et illustrati superna gracia tandem ad verum, quod Christus est, lumen properent claritatis." Cf. a slightly earlier formula (1 January 1421): "Licet Iudeorum omnium quos S.R.E. tolerat in testimonium Christi nostri sit reprobanda perfidia, tamen ex divine voluntatis indulgencia et benignitate processit quod ipsis inter Christiani nominis professores vitam servilem ducere sit permissum ut illorum monitis et exemplis nostri discant redemptoris noticiam obtinere et viam agnoscere veritatis" (Archivio Segreto Vaticano, Reg. Vat. 347, f. 157v).

[54] For an example, see the *Summa Parisiensis* at dist. 45, in *The Summa Parisiensis on the Decretum Gratiani*, ed. Terence P. McLaughlin (Toronto, 1952), p. 40: "Quod hic dicitur de Judaeis intelligi simili modo potest de Saracenis ... sive sunt Saraceni sive Judaei, dum rebelles fuerint, debemus eos persequi. Postquam vero eos subjugaverimus, neque interficere, nec ad fidem cogere debemus."

[55] Cited below, p. 47, note 70; on the treatment of this text by canonists, see Peter Herde, "Christians and Saracens at the Time of the Crusades: Some Comments of Contemporary Canonists," *Studia Gratiana* 12 (1967) 359–376. Popular theories on the permanent enmity with Saracens abounded. For example, the Lord allowed Saracens to

As sharp as it was, this distinction would often become blurred as western Christendom came to embrace an increasing number of Muslim communities. To govern relations with their inhabitants it was natural enough to use as a model what legislation existed about Jews. The problems seemed similar and suggested similar solutions: separate quarters, distinguishing clothing, the prohibition of employing Christian servants, no fraternization, no holding of public office, and so on. Conversely, the differences between them seemed of little moment. This was a mode of thought made explicit in the thirteenth century when laws respecting Jews and Saracens were lumped together into a single *quaestio* of Gregory IX's *Decretals*, entitled "De iudaeis, sarracenis, et eorum servis."

The blurring of distinctions between Jews and Saracens was not simply a matter of convenience. It was rooted in a biblical imagery at once commonplace and vivid. More than once, in the documents that follow, Oldradus mentions the Saracens as being descendants of Hagar, the Egyptian slave girl who was Sarah's handmaiden. This was part of a typology that saw in Abraham's wife Sarah the Catholic church, and in her slave Hagar "the accursed sect of Muhammad," as Islam was often called.[56] This typology had a long history, going back at least to Josephus who would elaborate on the story of Genesis 16 when Sarah told Abraham to go into her handmaiden Hagar, which was bound to spell trouble: how Hagar the Egyptian slave girl, large with Abraham's child, queened it over her barren mistress; how Sarah complained to Abraham, who told her that Hagar was her slave to do with as she wished; how Hagar, now beaten and humiliated at Sarah's hand, fled into the desert where an angel of the Lord told her that her misfortunes were the result of her own pride and sent her back, adding that she would bear a son whose hand would be raised against all men, and against whom the hands of all men would be raised in turn; how she gave birth to Ishmael; how Sarah at first welcomed the child but later, after she herself had borne Isaac, nagged Abraham until he finally packed Hagar and Ishmael off to the desert where they nearly perished, but where

---

exist so that Christians could gain merit by warring against them: "Sicut ergo reges sustinent fieri torneamenta in regnis suis propter militum excercitationem, ita et dominus permittit istos adversarios Sarracenos esse in mundo ut fideles se cum eis excercitando in bello merita sibi accumulent" (Humbert of Romans, *De predicatione crucis*, Vat. Lat. 3847, f. 8vb, which Dr. Penny Cole, University of Toronto, kindly called to my attention).

[56] Below, Cons. 72; or "conventicula haereticorum" according to the *glossa ordinaria* on Gratian, C. 23 q. 4 c. 39.

God promised Hagar that great things were in store for her son. Later still, Josephus says, Abraham gave Ishmael the land of Arabia.[57]

The elements that tie Hagar's son Ishmael to the Arabs and Islam are clear: the expulsion into the waste land, there to wander without fixed home; Abraham's bequest of Arabia; an Islam at war against all, Persian, Syrian, Byzantine, African, European; finally, the promise of a great future. No wonder, then, that in an Islamic tradition where Abraham already occupied a prominent place, his son Ishmael would come to loom large in the legends surrounding the Kaaba in Mecca, and achieve prominence as the ancestor of the northern Arabs and therefore of the Arabized tribes in general.[58] Nor was this peculiar to Islamic tradition alone. In Jewish biblical exegesis Ishmaelite had long been a synonym for Arab, and soon became so for Muslim. It was the same in the later exegesis of western Christendom, but there the character of Ishmael took on a sinister note—Ishmael the outcast, Ishmael the homeless wanderer and, especially after the rapid expansion of Islam in the seventh and eighth centuries, Ishmael the destroyer, at war with all mankind.[59] For Bede, who recorded the Saracen[60] attacks on Gaul in the eighth century, the words that the angel of the Lord spoke to Hagar in the desert provided only too accurate a description of the destroyer of Gaul, whose hand was raised against all men, and against whom the hands of all men were raised in turn.[61] It was

[57] Josephus, *The Jewish Antiquities*, 1.186–190, 215–219, 2.213; trans. H. St.J. Thackeray *et al.*, Loeb Classical Library, 9 vols. (London, 1926–1965), 4:93, 105–109, 257.

[58] See Rudi Paret, "Ismāʿīl" in *Encyclopedia of Islam* 4 (1978) 184–185.

[59] The identification of Ishmael with Saracens had been transmitted to the West through Jerome; cf. Jerome's commentary on Genesis (PL 23:1012): "Hic erit rusticus homo. 'Manus eius super omnes, et manus omnium super eum, et contra faciem omnium fratrum suorum habitabit.' Pro rustico in Hebraeo scriptum habet PHARA, quod interpretatur *onager*. Significat autem semen eius habitaturum in eremo, id est Saracenos vagos, incertisque sedibus, qui universas gentes quibus desertum ex latere jungitur incursant, et impugnantur ab omnibus." Cf. Marbury B. Ogle, "Petrus Comestor, Methodius, and the Saracens," *Speculum* 21 (1946) 318–324.

[60] Christians knew the Ishmaelites as "Saracens." Isidore of Seville gave the term increased currency in the West: "Ismael filius Abraham, a quo Ismaelitae, qui nunc corrupto nomine Saraceni, quasi a Sarra, et Agareni ab Agar"; see his *Etymologies* 9.2.6, in *Isidori Hispalensis episcopi Etymologiarum sive originum libri xx*, ed. W.M. Lindsay, 1 (unpaginated); see also 9.2.57: "Saraceni dicti, vel quia ex Sarra genitos se praedicent, vel sicut gentiles aiunt, quod ex origine Syrorum sint, quasi Syriginae. Hi peramplam habitant solitudinem. Ipsi sunt et Ismaelitae, ut liber Geneseos docet, quod sint ex Ismaele. ... Ipsi Agareni ab Agar; qui, ut diximus, perverso nomine Saraceni vocantur, quia ex Sarra se genitos gloriantur."

[61] Gen 16: "Hic erit ferus homo, manus eius contra omnes, et manus omnium contra eum, et e regione universorum fratrum suorum figet tabernacula." Cf. Bede, *Libri quatuor in principium genesis usque ad nativitatem Isaac et eiectionem Ismahelis adnotationum* xvi.12,

from Ishmael that the hated nation of the Saracens must have taken their rise: they were followers of the cult of Satan, special adversaries of the church raised up by God to invade Europe in order to punish the people of Spain, Provence and Burgundy for their fornications.[62]

But, strangely enough, alongside this picture of Hagar mother of the Saracens the West preserved another, of Hagar the Synagogue. In his letter to the Galatians, Paul contrasted the freedom of the new covenant with the slavery of the old by depicting the story of Hagar and Sarah as an allegory of the old and new testaments.[63] As Hagar had been a bondwoman, so too was the Jerusalem of this world; as Sarah had been free so also was the "Jerusalem which is above." The text was not lost on early pagan converts to Christianity among whom allegorizing the Hebrew bible had become a favourite pastime. Scorned by the Jews as children of Esau, they threw the taunt back at their tormentors. In so doing, they created for the future a typology of Christianity = Isaac = Jacob as opposed to Synagogue = Ishmael = Esau.[64] Thus it was that Hagar, from whom descended the Saracens, became, on Paul's authority, the Synagogue.

Slaves Reproved by the Lord

One way of dealing with the seeming confusion of these various figures is to see in the two women, Sarah and Hagar, biblical allegories of Church and Synagogue, but in their sons, Isaac and Ishmael, prototypes of the historical reality of Christendom and Islam, in this way applying to the mothers an allegorical, to the sons a literal reading of biblical history,[65] both traditional forms of biblical interpretation. Indeed, Bede's view of the Saracens lends some support to this, the literal view of a down-to-earth historian who needs no allegory to explain hard facts: long ago the Saracens had been desert wanderers, driven out by all; now, in the eighth

---

in *Bedae Venerabilis opera* 2.1, ed. Charles W. Jones, Corpus christianorum, series latina 118A (Turnhout: Brepols, 1967), p. 201.

[62] On all of which see Charles Plummer's notes to *Historia ecclesiastica* 5.23, in *Venerabilis Baedae opera historica* (Oxford, 1896) 2:339.

[63] Gal 4:22–26.

[64] See Gerson D. Cohen, "Esau as Symbol in Early Medieval Thought," in *Jewish Medieval and Renaissance Studies*, ed. Alexander Altmann, Philip W. Lown Institute of Advanced Judaic Studies, Brandeis University, Studies and Texts 4 (Cambridge, Mass. 1967), 19–48.

[65] See R.W. Southern, *Western Views of Islam in the Middle Ages* (Cambridge, Mass., 1962), pp. 16–17.

century, they bring war and destruction to everyone, having overrun all of Africa, most of Asia, and a good part of Europe. It was a view that would later be widely disseminated in the West by Peter Comestor.[66]

But in the medieval literature about Sarah and Hagar, Ishmael and Isaac, no one seems to have made any such neat distinction, nor indeed thought that any distinction was needed. Isidore of Seville occasionally fused the two traditions; he used Ishmael and Isaac not to represent Islam and Christendom, but to symbolize the peoples of the old and new testament, Jew and Christian: two peoples "... ex utroque testamento procedentes ... ."[67] Yet he felt no discomfort in also labelling Ishmael a Saracen, and (in his commentary on Genesis) likening Hagar to the Synagogue.[68] This kind of conflation persisted into the later Middle Ages. Oldradus betrays no sense of incongruity, for example, when he describes Muslims, Hagar's children, as "slaves reproved by the Lord," citing in support a decretal in which Jews were condemned to servitude because of the crucifixion. His mind easily slips from Jew to Muslim, from Muslim to Jew, reflecting the double character of their common mother. The persistence of this double character, these two Hagars, suggests something beyond mere allegory; rather, we seem to have here a reflection of one of the primary functions of biblical history, the function of prophecy, that is, the revelation of divine providence: the prophecy fulfilled, Hagar the Synagogue brought low; the prophecy yet to be fulfilled, Hagar mother of Ishmael the Saracen, soon also to be brought low.[69]

To look at it in this way may help us to understand the lumping together of Jew and Muslim which remains characteristic of the fourteenth century. To be sure, this was the consequence of practical problems having to do

[66] Peter Comestor, whom Oldradus would cite (see below, Cons. 72), drew on a pseudo-Methodius, the Latin text of whose work goes back to the eighth century (edited by Ernst Sackur, *Sybillinische Texte und Forschungen: Pseudo-Methodius, Adso, und die tiburtinische Sybille* [Halle, 1898]). See also Paul J. Alexander, "Byzantium and the Migration of Literary Works and Motifs: The Legend of the Last Roman Emperor," *Medievalia et Humanistica*, new series 2 (1971) 47–68; and Otto Prinz, "Eine frühe abendländische Aktualisierung der lateinischen Übersetzung des Pseudo-Methodius," *Deutsches Archiv für Erforschung des Mittelalters* 41 (1985) 1–23.

[67] *Allegoriae* (PL 83:104–105).

[68] PL 83:248: "Quod vero in solitudine errat Agar cum filio suo, significat Synagogam cum populo suo expulsam de terra sua ... ."

[69] Cf. Innocent III's call for a crusade in 1213 (PL 216:818): "... quidam perditionis filius, Machometus pseudopropheta, surrexit, ... cujus perfidia etsi usque ad haec tempora invaluerit; confidimus tamen in Domino, qui jam fecit nobiscum signum in bonum, quod finis hujus bestiae appropinquat, cujus numerus secundum Apocalypsin Joannis intra sexcenda [sic] sexaginta sex clauditur, ex quibus jam pene sexcenti sunt anni completi."

with the political and social treatment of both peoples, but it nevertheless demanded, as so much else in the West, a theological justification to be acceptable. It is precisely here that Oldradus will leave aside for the moment his legal sources and quote the theologian Peter Comestor, one-time chancellor of the University of Paris, on Ishmael as the father of Islam (Muslims); and then in the same sentence, the same breath so to speak, cite a legal gloss calling Ishmael's mother the Synagogue whose descendants (Jews) ought to be the servants of those who descend from Sarah (Christians). Here, at the level of servitude, Oldradus joins Jew and Muslim: the Jew, child of Hagar the Synagogue, to be tolerated only as a matter of grace because of Hagar's ingratitude to Sarah;[70] the Saracen, child of Hagar the accursed handmaiden, now to be beaten as Sarah had once beaten Hagar herself.[71]

One of the oddest of Oldradus' consilia discusses the legality of a conversion of a Jew to Islam, a conversion from one religion to another the distinctions between which he probably knew very little about and cared about even less, as being beside the point. He puts it quite succinctly: we tolerate both sects; if each is in a state of damnation it does not matter to which one belongs because there is no distinction between equivalents.[72] We seem to be in the presence here of an ingrained realism obscuring the unique identities of, and blending into a single class, all those outside Catholicism, among whom the only distinctions worth noting are their respective relations to orthodox Christianity.[73] All the stronger, therefore, the propensity for grouping Jews and Muslims together, despite their myriad differences. Both were outside the Christian community, both

[70] Cons. 87: "For when they abuse our grace the ungrateful deserve to lose their privilege."

[71] Cons. 72.

[72] Cons. 51: "Si utrobique sit in statu damnationis non est curandum in qua earum sit quia non refert quid ex equipollentibus fiat." It is difficult to imagine how a case of this nature might have come up, and it is tempting to think of it as some sort of exercise or theoretical discussion. Nevertheless, such conversions could not have been uncommon, especially in the Spanish peninsula. Cf. Jean Régné, *History of the Jews in Aragon: Regesta and Documents 1213–1327* (Jerusalem, 1978), p. 153, nos. 847 (1280) and 848 (1280): three Jews tried for abandoning Judaism in favour of Islam; p. 212, no. 1171 (1284): death sentence for a Jewish convert from Islam named Maulet, for returning to Islam. For a general discussion of Jewish conversion to Islam in Spain, including a discussion of this consilium, see William C. Stalls, "Jewish Conversion to Islam: The Perspective of a *Quaestio*," *Revista Española de Teologia* 43 (1983) 235–251.

[73] One might therefore use a text about Christian slaves in the pagan households of antiquity to illustrate an equivalence of Jew, pagan (Muslim) and heretic (below, p. 42, note 32). Also, as with the heretic, neither the Jew nor the Muslim could take sanctuary in a church (Cons. 54).

members of developed religions that each in one way or another rivalled Christianity. Jews or Saracens, they could best be perceived in their relationship to Christians, in peace or at war, passive or troublesome, silent or scandalous. To the extent that Muslims, like Jews, were prepared to serve everywhere, to that extent they might be looked upon as akin to Jews.

And so Oldradus will freely apply to Muslims descriptions of Jews, calling them "slaves reproved by the Lord," using the very words, now long enshrined in the *Decretals*, that Innocent III had used for Jews alone as being responsible for the crucifixion. Again, when discussing the legitimacy of war against Muslims in Spain, Oldradus cites a decretal about not compelling Jews to be baptized, so extending to Muslims a tolerance derived from the opinion, repeated from the time of St. Augustine on, that Jews who cause no trouble should be left in peace.[74]

Saracens in Western Law

Clearly, defining the proper relations between Christians and Muslims demanded the use of laws about Jews.[75] From the beginning of the thirteenth century Jews received more and more legislative attention, while there remained a paucity of legal texts bearing directly on Muslims.[76] There is no mystery in this; there was nothing in the bare confrontation of Islam and Christianity to compare with the rich historical ties between Jews and Christians, no place in western thought for Muslims that could rival the unique role defined for Jews in Christian tradition. Islam was simply an enemy with whom war was a duty, peace unthinkable. From time to time Saracens might hide their hostile intentions out of some necessity, but they would snatch at every opportunity to achieve their wicked ends, as Clement IV would remind James I of Aragon in 1266.[77] Even during periods of truce with Islamic states, the tension between Christians and those Muslims who lived within Christian territory remained severe. Every effort was made to

[74] Oldradus could find support in the *Cod.*, 1.11.6, stipulating that peaceful Jews and pagans were not to be attacked by Christians–pagans here meaning Saracens (see below, p. 42, note 31).

[75] Cf. Henri Gilles, "Législation et doctrine canoniques sur les Sarrasins," *Islam et chrétiens du Midi (xiie–xive s.)*, Cahiers de Fanjeaux 18 (Toulouse, 1983), pp. 195–213.

[76] Cf. the discussion in Herde, "Christians and Saracens at the Time of the Crusades," pp. 362–363.

[77] "... qui licet ad tempus occultent iniquitatis suae necessitate cogente propositum, illud tamen quam avide, quam ardenter, imo etiam quam inique captata opportunitate revelant." Baronius, *Annales ecclesiastici*, Clem. IV, an. 1226, §29). The accusation was a commonplace, echoed by Oldradus below, Cons. 72.

curtail commerce with Muslim communities in the Mediterranean, and the enslavement and extinction of Muslims in Sicily and southern Italy continued. Relations with Muslims in the Holy Land before its loss were circumscribed; they were equally limited in Spain, where Muslim communities were barely tolerated, carefully held at arms length, and where the occasional employment of Muslims in public office never failed to scandalize church authorities.

Under the circumstances, there was little chance for any coherent development of legal thought about social relations with Muslims. To the extent that Jews and Muslims might be treated alike, it was convenient for any laws respecting the one to be used to justify the treatment of the other. That is why, when Oldradus was asked to deal with the question of expulsion of Jews and Saracens, almost all the arguments he could muster on either side of the question he would take from laws about Jews.[78] He could have found little else in formal canon law to help. What Gratian's *Decretum* had on Muslims was slight, and that reminiscent of an earlier day: long standing proscription against carrying arms to the Saracens; Pope Alexander II's bald declaration that Saracens were enemies against whom war was licit. Gregory IX's *Decretals*[79] added little more: again, strictures about trading in war contraband with the Saracen enemy, drawn from the canons of Lateran III and IV; prohibitions of Muslims' or Jews' keeping Christian servants; prohibition of their holding public office; the requirement of Lateran IV that both wear distinctive clothing. Boniface VIII's *Sext* added nothing. The *Clementines* contained one canon of Clement V's Council of Vienne[80] about the scandal caused by Muslims living in Christian communities, caused by the public call by the muezzin to prayer in their mosques where they "adore" Muhammad and by the pilgrimage of great masses of Saracens to worship at his grave, both matters that Christian authorities henceforth were called upon to put a stop to.[81]

To deal with the question of expulsion, Oldradus had more than decretal collections to lean on. There were the legal commentators who, when dealing with Saracens, gave most of their attention to the question implicitly raised by Alexander II's dictum: if to attack Saracens was licit because they persecuted Christians, how were they to be dealt with when

[78] Below, Cons. 87.

[79] For the *Compilationes antiquae*, which for the most part included elements that would eventually find a place in the *Decretals*, see Herde, "Christians and Saracens at the Time of the Crusades," p. 363.

[80] Promulgated by John XXII in 1317.

[81] *Clem.* 5.2.un.

they did not? The problem was not a simple one. Although it was legitimate to war against Muslims who belonged to an Islamic, and therefore an enemy state, the texts of canon law said nothing at all about how they were to be treated as individuals living within a Christian state. In the course of time, as the Christian frontier in Spain was pushed forward and a growing number of Muslim communities were overrun, this was the question that legal commentators had frequently to address. Almost to a man they responded by adopting rules applicable to Jews: provided that Saracens, like Jews, were obedient and peaceful, caused no trouble and did not proselytize, they were to be tolerated.[82]

The most explicit of these comparisons had been made quite early, by the author of the twelfth-century *Summa* "Permissio quedam," commenting on Alexander II's sharp distinction: it would seem that "Saracens are worse than Jews, but this should not be understood in such a simple sense, for just as we might be provoked by Saracens, so we might also by Jews; and just as we ought not to deprive Jews of their goods, so too Saracens. What is said here [by Alexander] is said because of the way Saracens are accustomed to act. If Jews were to do the same, we should be warring with them."[83] The doctrine, therefore, was one of long standing: if Saracens living among us conform as do the Jews, they are to be treated in the same way.

In this way commentators fleshed out the skeletal provisions of canon law to be found within the section "De iudaeis, sarracenis, et eorum servis."[84] Occasionally they also took the opportunity, even when commenting on other parts of the *Decretals*, to elaborate on questions of Jews and Saracens. For example, a question on baptism led Pope Innocent IV, in his own commentary on the *Decretals*, to throw in a passing remark to the effect that although war against Muslims was licit when they invaded Christian lands, or held the Holy Land, Christians ought not to war against them if there was a chance of their conversion.[85] And it was in his comment on a decretal in the section dealing with vows that he made his major contribution to the whole question of relations with infidels, which quickly became the *locus classicus*. In effect, Innocent provided the definitive justification both for Christian claims to the Holy Land and for

[82] Herde, "Christians and Saracens at the Time of the Crusades," pp. 364–373.

[83] Ibid, p. 367, note 29.

[84] Book 5, title 6.

[85] X, 3.5.4 : "... ex his ergo apparet Sarracenis, ut fiant Christiani, bellum indicendum non esse ... ."

papal claims to authority over non-Christians, setting the direction to be taken by all subsequent discussion.[86]

Laws about Jews were not the only resource for defining the relations of Christians and Muslims. By assimilating Muslims to "pagans," one could apply to them many texts in the *Decretum* and in Justinian's *Codex* drawn for the most part from sources dealing with non-Christians in late antiquity.[87] More important still—probably not to lawyers like Oldradus, but certainly, in a practical sense, to the life of Muslim communities—was the role played by local legislation. Although after 1291 Christians no longer lived cheek by jowl with Muslims in the Holy Land, there were large numbers of Muslims in the West—in Sicily, for example, where despite mass emigration and slaughter there were many sunk in a life of servitude.[88] There the word *agarenus*, derived from Hagar, widely used as a synonym for Muslim, had acquired a secondary meaning, *villein*.[89] More important, there remained a huge 'Saracen problem' localized along a fluid frontier within the Spanish peninsula. There Muslims lived uneasily within Christian kingdoms that were often at war with Islamic states. In some

[86] X, 3.34.8, s.v. *Pro defensione terrae sanctae.*

[87] For example, *Codex* 1.11.6, to demonstrate that Muslims were a tolerated sect: "Christianis ... demandamus ut Iudaeis ac paganis in quiete degentibus ... non audeant manus inferre religionis auctoritate abusi"; and see Emilio Bussi, "La condizione giuridica dei musulmani nel diritto canonico," *Rivista di storia del diritto italiano* 8 (1935) 459–494. Calling Arabs pagans was a practice of long standing; for example, see Pope John VIII in PL 126:708 (ep. 55 ad Guaiferium).

[88] Cf. Denis Mack Smith, *A History of Sicily: Medieval Sicily 800–1713* (London, 1968), pp. 59–60.

[89] E. Curtis, *Roger of Sicily and the Normans in Lower Italy 1016–1154* (New York and London, 1917), p. 419, cited in Aziz Ahmad, *A History of Islamic Sicily* (Edinburgh, 1975), p. 69. The custom that freedom was to be granted to slaves upon Christian baptism had long been abrogated. See, for example, Gregory IX's letter to his legate, the patriarch of Jerusalem, in 1227, about slaves who were being denied baptism because it was thought this was a pretence to win personal freedom, and because even churchmen and religious were unwilling to lose slaves through the sacrament of baptism: "Verum cum ex hoc, non absque Redemptoris offensa et scandalo timentium Dominum, nimis saluti depereat animarum, mandamus quatenus illos ex sclavis eisdem, qui pure et simpliciter propter Deum adscribi fidelium collegio cupiunt et deposcunt, in servitute pristina permansuri, baptizari libere permittatis ..."; Aloysius L. Tàutu, *Acta Honorii III et Gregorii IX*, Fontes, ser. III, vol. 3 (Vatican City, 1950), pp. 307–308 (no. 228). The best that Hostiensis could do was suggest that masters should treat their slaves more leniently after they were baptized; cf. Kedar, *Crusade and Mission*, pp. 146–150. Frederick III of Trinacria (Sicily), in a constitution on Jews and Muslims in 1310, was still reprimanding slave owners who were preventing the conversion of their Muslim slaves (see Finke, *Acta Aragonensia* 2:695–699).

areas Muslims peopled whole villages exclusively.[90] In others, the *morería* was a common feature of many Spanish towns. Laws dealing with these communities therefore tended to be local enactments of secular authorities, providing for the economic and social organization of Muslim subjects in a Christian state: their religious rights and practices, judicial structures, taxation, local government and the like. Sometimes local regulations reflected general church directives, especially those having to do with dress, intermarriage and servants. There were also attempts, not always successful, to force Muslims to pay the tithe required by canon law, even on lands that had not hitherto been held by Christians.[91] But for the most part the regulation of Christian-Saracen relations remained a local matter which, in Spain at least, had as its purpose the political containment of newly conquered peoples.

Coexistence

One of Oldradus' consilia touched on the problem of the relationship of Christians and Muslims in no comprehensive way, but only in response to the question whether to avail oneself of the help of an 'infidel' (or possibly, who knows? to enter into some local alliance with Muslims) might be a sin. It was a practical question, no doubt, given conditions in Spain at the time, but not one to stimulate a profound study of a general problem. He approved, leaning heavily on the Roman legal principle of self-defence. To use the help of an infidel was akin to, and as licit as, using deceit and other such means in warfare, acceptable provided the ends were just—if, in other words, it were a 'just war.'[92] No real foundation here for coexistence. Furthermore, despite the tendency to treat Jews and Muslims alike, the conflation of Jew and Muslim was always tempered by one clear mark of distinction: the existence of a permanent state of war with Islam. Alexander II's decretal *dispar* defined Muslims as *ipso facto* persecutors of Christians, whereas Jews were "ubique servire parati." Some might be willing to tolerate a peaceful Muslim state as a neighbour. Not so Oldradus, and not so the Muslim states of Spain. If they are now at peace, it is only because they see no way of doing injury. Even should they wish to live in permanent peace, this would still be intolerable. To attack them

[90] Cf. Karl W. Butzer, Elizabeth K. Butzer, Juan F. Mateu, "Medieval Muslim Communities of the Sierra de Espadan, Kingdom of Valencia," *Viator* 17 (1986) 348.

[91] John Boswell, *The Royal Treasure: Muslim Communities under the Crown of Aragon in the Fourteenth Century* (New Haven, 1977), p. 200. Cf. Cons. 91 below.

[92] Below, Cons. 71.

no matter what the circumstances is justified, for they are the children of Ishmael. It is Hagar herself that must be driven out. "The Holy Church, symbolized by Sarah, will therefore use that accursed handmaiden [Hagar] ... as her Lord commands, by driving her out and depriving her children of inheritance and possession, that they not share with the free children."[93]

But when asked whether Muslims should be required to pay tithes to the Christian church, or should be driven from their native villages, Oldradus was in fact handed an opportunity to range over the question of Christian-Muslim relations in far more general terms. His reply in the matter of tithes clearly assumed permanent settlements of Muslims within Christian lands. The question of expulsion, in fact, was directed at both Jews and Muslims. We have no clue as to who posed the question, or at what moment or in relation to what set of events it came up. It undoubtedly points to some part of Spain where the question of the expulsion of Muslim communities was real and pressing. There is nothing original about the material that Oldradus uses; his sources are the usual ones, handled in the usual ways. But it is worth noting that he wrote two consilia on the question, not one. The second, Cons. 264, seems to have been his contribution to a general consilium which included the conflicting opinions of other consultants. Clearly, the subject was a troubling one, and must have come up more than once.

A comparison of the two consilia in which he discussed the question is indeed instructive. The first, Cons. 87, has an air of impartiality achieved in the standard way: first come the arguments on the one side, for leaving Jews and Saracens in peace, then on the other, for driving them out. Nor are the arguments against expelling Jews and Saracens trivial. Those that were based on laws touching on Saracens included reference to the provision in Justinian's *Codex* about not harming Jews and pagans (= Saracens) who caused no trouble. They also included reference to the provision, also to be found in the *Codex*, guaranteeing the security of title to all who had acquired property from the state. Oldradus even dredged up John Chrysostom's remark, cited by Gratian, to the effect that Christians might eat at the same table as pagans, a text explained by the glossator as being intended to win them to the Christian faith.

In the main, however, Oldradus had to use laws about Jews alone to argue against the expulsion of both Jews and Saracens. These included the classic provisions that had been developed to protect Jewish communities:

[93] Gal 4:30. For *dispar*, see below, p. 47, note 70. Cf. Herde, "Christians and Saracens at the Time of the Crusades," pp. 364–368.

Jews were not to be forcibly baptized; they could repair their synagogues when necessary (though not build new ones); they were not to be despoiled of their goods provided they were peaceable; in perpetual servitude, they served an important purpose in the history of the human race, a "perverse people ... marked, not to be slain, but rather to be tolerated."

All of which might be used to prohibit popular persecution of Jews or Saracens. It was quite another matter, however, when it came to the right of a ruler to confiscate the property of or to expel "especially the Jews." Now Oldradus reverted to the definition of Jews as chattels of the public authority, based on the role defined for them as perpetual servants, enslaved by the emperor Constantine: "for they were made slaves through the death of Christ." Their toleration, therefore, was a matter of grace, of Christian piety, not of law or right. This was especially true where they might prove to be troublesome. The fact that Oldradus would make such an argument, appropriate to Jews alone, in a discussion presumably applicable to Muslims also, is in itself a measure of the assimilation of Jews and Muslims in western thought.

The last part of the consilium dealt with the question of the pope's role in urging or allowing that Jews and Saracens be driven out, their goods taken from them. Although Oldradus held that princes had a clear right to expel them, he added that the pope should not encourage princes to exercise such a right where Jews (now no mention of Saracens) create no scandal and live quietly. At the very end of the consilium, however, he recalled two letters of Pope Gregory I, one increasing the assessment of pagan rustics (= Saracens?) in order to hasten their conversion to Christianity, the other remitting the assessments of Jews to the same end. If this suggests that he thought that the treatment of the two peoples should be different, that Muslims should be treated more harshly than Jews, he was clearly unwilling to make the point explicit, or to pursue the argument any further. In fact, the entire consilium, though striking an assertive tone, remains curiously inconclusive.

The contrast with Cons. 264 is remarkable. Oldradus seems to have written this consilium as part of a joint consultation embracing the advice of others among whom, to judge from his opening sentence, there was some difference of opinion. He himself aimed at a *modus vivendi* for Muslims within Christian territory by basing it on the long established model of the Jews. While not neglecting Jews, he addressed the question of Muslims more directly than he had in Cons. 87. Moreover, he no longer emphasized the rights of the prince. Instead, he was concerned to limit the occasion for the exercise of such rights: the prince is not to expel peaceful Jews and Saracens without cause.

And the law on which the arguments were now based?

First, the fundamental law of nature, which Oldradus equated with divine law revealed in the Gospel, although here cited from Gratian's *Decretum* and the canons of the *Decretals*: one must do unto others what one would wish done to oneself. This was as applicable to princes as to anyone else. Then, too, there was the divine law to love our neighbour, which includes Jews and Saracens who share our nature as human beings, for all of which the law of the church provided no lack of authoritative texts. Moreover, Gratian's *Decretum* also taught that not even the pope himself could dispense from such a law of nature.

Furthermore, there was the simple appeal to humanity. Just as we should show mercy to captives taken from an enemy, so should we be merciful to captive slaves, to be treated respectfully, out of charity, not cruelly in uncontrolled rage. They ought not to be despoiled either of their goods or of their homes. They hold their possessions by law—either by the law of nations, i.e. natural law, or by some legal title under human justice. Where they misuse or abuse their privileges they may indeed be expelled; but by the same token, if they do not, they may not.

In all of this we are sent to canon laws that do not speak to Jews or Saracens alone, but generally to the condition of humankind. Oldradus briefly breaks off, however, to consider Saracens directly, and does so through a familiar medium. Sarah (Christianity) drove off Hagar and Ishmael (Islam) because they persecuted Sarah and Isaac. It follows that if they do not persecute the Christian church, if they refrain from injuring Christians, give no trouble, and do not mislead Christians as to the true faith, they are to be tolerated, not expelled. Christ committed both pagans and Jews to St.Peter and his successors to be nourished. Infidels (a stock term for Saracens) were not to be treated harshly, but led to the faith with kindness; Oldradus passed over in silence the fact that the canonical text he used in support of this referred to Jews alone.

Muslims who offend are to be dealt with under the law, not by expulsion. While war against a Muslim state is justified, Muslims living among us are not to be expelled or punished without cause. They are not to lose their possessions. They ought not to be driven from the communities where they were born. We ought not to injure those who conduct themselves peaceably. If *dispar* refers to those who persecute Christians, then it ought not to apply to those who do not.

If at first sight Oldradus seems now to have changed an earlier opinion, strictly viewed his two consilia are complementary: Cons. 87 established the right of the prince to expel, Cons. 264 merely defined the reasons why he should not do so.[94] Nor was there anything new about these reasons. They represented common legal opinion. What was new is that the argument was taken out of the classroom and applied to a pressing situation, a Christian society on a war footing in which the toleration of Muslim and Jewish minorities was not only conceivable, but indeed desirable. What is intriguing in all this is that the argument almost imperceptibly tended to blend Jew and Muslim. In brief, the Muslim who accepted the position of the Jew, who gave no trouble, caused no scandal, and was "prepared to serve everywhere," could enjoy the same legal protection.

Damnata Commixtio

Only one of these consilia dealt with an actual court case. It had to do with sexual relations between Christian and non-Christian, an unnamed Christian woman and a Jew named Pandonus.[95] The case was heard by the royal court of Avignon, for the city was still in the possession of the crown of Naples. Oldradus did not include his consilium on the case in his original collection. It was one of those turned up by a later editor. It remains the best known and most widely cited of all his consilia, for reasons that will become obvious.[96]

The consilium is of some historical interest because it refers to an otherwise unknown privilege given to the Jews of Avignon by a certain Queen M. This might refer to Mary of Burgundy (d. 1308), the second wife of Charles I (d. 1285), or Mary of Hungary, the wife of Charles II. The only knowledge we have of the contents of the privilege comes from the rather

[94] There is no external evidence as to which of these two consilia was written before the other. The nature of the discussion and the legal citations of each suggest the relationship adopted above; the slightly "unedited" form of Cons. 264, the last of the original collection, with its indication of being part of a consilium prepared with other advocates, would also seem to support this.

[95] For a fifteenth-century consilium on the same subject, which rehearses many of the points that here follow, and which also cites Oldradus among others, see Vatican City, Biblioteca Vaticana, MS Urb. Lat. 1132, ff. 363v–364v: "Judeus cognoscens christianam qua pena sit puniendus in terminis iuris communis quando delictum est consummatum."

[96] Oldradus may have been acting for the accused, or may have been consulted by the court. For evidence that Jews in Provence had access to legal consultations, professional consilia, see Joseph Shatzmiller, *Recherches sur la communauté juive de Manosque au moyen âge (1241–1329)* (Paris, 1973), pp. 96–97.

obscure language of the consilium itself, which seems to imply that what was said under torture should not form part of the instruction of the court.[97] We might note that Robert, who succeeded Charles II as king of Sicily and Count of Provence, would denounce those of his judges who used torture: no one was to be "put to the question" other than those who had already been guilty of some serious offence.[98] This is the rule that seems to be reflected in what Oldradus has to say about the case.

Turning to the substance of the case itself, it is a well known fact that the marriage of Jew and Christian in the Middle Ages was defined in law as "adultery," for which the penalty could be severe. It was precisely this charge of adultery that Oldradus tried to get reduced. Since it was the act of marriage of Jew and Christian which constituted adultery in law, casual sexual relations between them, he argued, did not, unless accompanied by an overt act or contract of marriage, absent from this case.[99] He also leaned heavily on the argument having to do with the limitation of torture: although forced to make a confession, Pandonus confessed only to trivial matters and not to any past criminal activity.[100] The procedure had

[97] For a privilege providing that Jews not be "put to the question," i.e. tortured to give evidence, see the statute of James I of Aragon respecting the Jews of Montpellier, 1 February 1267, in an obviously problematical reading: "... quod aliquis ex ipsis judeis aliqua causa vel ratione in judicium deducta vel non deducta non questionetur nec questionari possit nec alicui eorum fiat vel incuciatur(!) aliquo tempore facto sine (sive?) dicto timor vel terror questionis nisi sub hac forma producto enim judicio vel inquistione incepto incepto vel incepto contra judeum usque ad finem"; and again on 17 June 1274, in a slightly more intelligible version: "Cum nos dederimus et concesserimus judeis nostris tam masculis quam feminis in parte nostra Montispesulani habitantibus et habitaturis quod aliquis ex ipsis judeis aliqua causa vel ratione in judicium deducta vel non deducta non questionetur nec questionari possit nec alicui eorum fiat vel ... tempore facto sive dicto timor vel ... questionis nisi sub certa forma in carta a nobis eis super hoc concessa plenius contenta et quod et inquisicionis non fiat nec fieri possit contra judeum ..." etc; Francisco de Bofarull, "Jaime I el conquistador y la comunidad judía de Montpeller," *Boletín de la Real Academia de Buenas Letras de Barcelona* 5 (1909–1910) 488, 491.

[98] Joseph Girard and P. Pansier, *La Cour temporelle d'Avignon aux xive et xve siècles* (Paris, 1909), p. 9; R. de Maulde, *Coutumes et règlements de la République d'Avignon au treizième siècle* (Paris, 1879), p. 315.

[99] It was an opinion shared by the author of a fifteenth-century consilium referred to above, p. 30, note 95. He cites Oldradus (Cons. 36) but does not cite this consilium on Pandonus, which he surely would have done if it had been part of the regular collection, not added later.

[100] He was forced ("tortus") to make some sort of confession. However, he only confessed to trivial matters ("tantum de vulgaribus confessus est"), not to any past criminal activity ("nullis iudiciis praecedentibus confessus fuit"), and therefore should not have been "put to the question." For some of the instruments of torture in the royal palace where all this went on, see Girard and Pansier, *La Cour temporelle d'Avignon*, p. 71 (no. XI, 6 March 1347).

contravened the privilege given to the Jews. Whatever Pandonus said, therefore, should not form part of the instruction of the court. Moreover, to judge from the texts of the *Digest* and *Codex* that he cited, having to do with women in taverns, women's dress as an indication of their place in society, and so on, Oldradus also tried to strengthen his case by disparaging the character of the woman involved. Finally, he made a strong plea for clemency on humanitarian grounds.

Despite his best arguments, however, the two judges who heard the case condemned Pandonus. They ordered his castration, the physical evidence of which, Oldradus tells us, he himself saw before the doors of the palace. It had been a difficult case, followed by an unusual sentence.[101] His disappointment may be measured by what he did next: he returned to his consilium and added to it the names of the two judges, Raymond of Apulia and Anthony "de Cruce," who had refused to listen to him.

[101] There is little to be found on castration as a judicial penalty in western law, but for an early pronouncement, which probably reflects a popular sense of justice, see the canons of the Council of Nablus (1120) on relations between Christians and Saracens in the crusader states, in Giovanni Domenico Mansi, *Sacrorum conciliorum nova et amplissima collectio ... editio novissima*, 31 vols. (Florence, 1759–1798) 21:264:

> cap. 12: Si quis cum consentiente sibi Saracena concubuisse probatus fuerit, ementuletur, illa vero naso truncetur.
> cap. 13: Si quis Saracenam suam vi oppresserit, ipsa quidem infiscabitur, ipse vero extestificabitur.
> cap. 14: Si quis Saracenam alterius vi supposuerit, similem sententiam subibit.
> cap. 15: Si Christiana Saraceno sponte commiscentur, ambo moechantium sententia judicentur. Si vero vi ab eo oppressa fuerit, ipsa quidem culpa non tenebitur, sed Saracenus eunuchizabitur.

THE CONSILIA

A Note on the Sources

Most of Oldradus' legal citations in the consilia that follow were made from texts of Roman and canon law and from the so-called ordinary glosses on those texts. For all such citations I have used standard editions: for canon law, E. Friedberg, *Corpus Iuris Canonici* (Leipzig, 2 vols. 1879–1881; rpt. Graz, 1959); for Roman law, Theodor Mommsen et al., *Corpus Iuris Civilis* (rpt. Graz, 3 vols. 1967–1970). Especially useful is the English translation of the *Digest* edited by Alan Watson (Philadelphia, 4 vols., 1985), which includes the Mommsen edition of the Latin text. For the *glossa ordinaria* on Gratian's *Decretum* by Johannes Teutonicus, later revised by Bartholomaeus of Brescia, I have used *Decretum Divi Gratiani totius prope modum iuris canonici compendium summorumque pontificum decreta ...* (Lyons, 1560); for the *glossa ordinaria* on Gregory IX's *Decretals* by Bernard of Parma, *Decretales D. Gregorii papae IX suae integritati una cum glossis restitutae* (Lyons, 1584); and for Accursius' *glossa ordinaria* on the *Codex* and *Digest* of Justinian, *Codicis sacratissimis imper. Iustiniani pp. Augusti lib. XII Accursii commentariis ... illustrati* (Geneva, 1625) and *Digestum Vetus D. Iustiniani sacratissimi principis ... cui praeter notissimos Accursii Florentini commentarios ... novae ... annotationes accesserunt, [Infortiatum ..., Digestum Novum ...]* (Lyons, 3 vols., 1549–1550).

The legal citations in the consilia tumble over one another in great profusion, creating many difficulties for the modern reader. They hinder the flow of the argument, their compressed and cryptic form can discourage the uninitiated, and they demand constant reference to legal authorities that are themselves difficult to handle. To ease the burden on the reader I have therefore removed all the citations from the following translations, placed them in separate notes, and cast them in modern form. I have frequently added a short selection from the legal text that Oldradus cited as an authority, or a summary (in English) of that text, or both, with citations from the relevant glosses where necessary. Whatever in the notes lies outside brackets [ ] is strictly Oldradus in translation. Whatever lies inside the brackets is either the text that he cited but did not himself quote, my summary of that text, an additional comment of my own, or some combination of all these. I have passed over in silence many small mistakes in attribution, probably the result of errors of transmission.

Consilium 36

Here follow articles of the Inquisitor of heresy in Romania.[1]

First, a certain Jew, who was baptized and became a Christian, remained a Christian for a long time. Later, he denied the faith of Christ and lapsed into Judaism. A certain Jew took him into his home, knowing him to be a Christian, kept him there for a long time, gave him a Jewish woman to wife, and so encouraged him in his Judaism.

Again, another Jew purchased a Christian boy whom he circumcised and caused to deny the Christian faith, having summoned for the purpose some other Jews who participated in the circumcision with him; and when the first Jew died, one of those who had been present at the circumcision took the boy and kept him for a long time. At length, fearing the Inquisition, he sent the boy to Alexandria to prevent his return to Christianity.

Again, this same Jew bought a Christian woman, whom he caused to become Jewish through denial of the Christian faith. He later married her and had two sons by her. Since the affair now was revealed to the Christians, he poisoned her. Moreover, the younger child, whom she was nursing, died with her. Later, after his own death, his executors sent the surviving son to Alexandria so that he could not be claimed by the Christians as being the son of a Christian woman.

Again, when a certain Jew had been accused of having been a Christian, and the Inquisitor was looking into it, another Jew made an agreement with the accused, for a certain price, that within a certain period of time he would rescue him from the hands of the Inquisitor, who was holding him under bond, and he did everything he could, by word, in writing, and by deed, and by arousing clerics and laymen against the Inquisitor, so that the latter was hardly able to find out the truth about the accused heretic.

Again, some Jews who had been baptized in various places came to the island of Crete and were living there as Jews. And when the Inquisitor was investigating them, some other Jews, who knew that they were Christians, so pestered them to leave the country in order to avoid arrest by the Inquisitor and a forced return to Christianity, that they were compelled to go, after getting from those Jews their transportation and expenses. When

[1] [Romania was the title attributed to the possessions of the eastern empire, "imperium Romanie," especially in and around the Aegean Sea. It continued to be used as a general descriptive term, even for territories in western hands such as Crete.]

he found out, the Inquisitor pursued them and arrested some of them; others escaped to Saracen lands.

Again, some Jews buy Christians, take them to Alexandria, and there sell them to Jews and Saracens, knowing full well that they force a denial of the faith of Christ.

Again, on Good Friday some Jews crucify a lamb or a sheep, and spit on the cross, and trample it underfoot in contempt of Jesus Christ.

The question is now put, how should one proceed against such people.

To the first article one replies that the Inquisitor will be able to proceed against such a Jew for being a harbourer of a heretic.[2] For, as a harbourer of a heretic he was a heretic.[3] The crime of harbouring is committed even if it is a single act,[4] to say nothing of this case where the act was carried out over a continuous period of time[5] and the harbourer was not content with just harbouring the person but arranged his marriage with a Jewish woman. It is evident that he encouraged him in the crime of Judaizing and of apostasy, which is the equivalent of heresy—lured him, rather, with a

[2] *Sext.*, 5.2.13 [Christians who return to Judaism are to be dealt with as heretics; their harbourers, as harbourers of heretics: "Contra Christianos qui ad ritum transierint vel redierint Iudaeorum, etiamsi huiusmodi redeuntes, dum erant infantes, aut mortis metu, non tamen absolute aut praecise coacti, baptizati fuerunt, erit tanquam contra haereticos, si fuerint de hoc confessi, aut per Christianos seu Iudaeos convicti, et sicut contra fautores, receptatores, et defensores haereticorum sic contra fautores, receptatores et defensores talium est procedendum"].

[3] *Dig.*, 47.16.1&2 [Who harbours a brigand is to be treated as a brigand: "Pessimum genus est receptatorum, sine quibus nemo latere diu potest; et praecipitur, ut perinde puniantur atque latrones"]. *Cod.*, 9.39 [A further elaboration of the same point; the "receptator" of a criminal is guilty of the same crime as the one he has protected and must expect the same punishment].

[4] For argument, *Dig.*, 48.5.30.4 [When a husband makes a profit from his wife's adultery, whether once or often is of no consequence: "Quaestum autem ex adulterio uxoris facere videtur, qui quid accepit ut adulteretur uxor: sive enim saepius sive semel accepit, non est eximendus ..."]; and this can be gathered from *Sext.*, 5.9.5 [A modification and reissue of the legislation of Honorius III against those who attacked or injured cardinals, or who knowingly received and protected such offenders].

[5] For argument, *Cod.*, 5.5.4 [This refers to penalties for those who marry in contravention of the law; the penalties may be waived later only if, when the error is finally discovered, it is corrected, i.e. the union is dissolved: "Quos tamen ita demum legis nostrae laqueis eximi placuit si aut errore comperto, aut ubi ad legitimos pervenirent annos, coniunctionem huiuscemodi sine ulla recrastinatione dirimerint"; otherwise, as the gloss adds: "alias dos et donatio propter nuptias confiscantur"].

persuasiveness that itself ought to be punished,[6] for such enticement goes beyond compulsion.[7]

If a Christian had done this it is certain that he could be prosecuted by the Inquisitor. Is he not to be excused, however, being a Jew? My answer is no, since by reason of the offence he becomes subject to the ecclesiastical court.[8] What of the argument that they [the Jews] are of no concern to us, being outsiders?[9] It is true that one can be compelled by excommunication; still, while excommunication expels one from the church, it has no place in the case of a Jew who is already outside the church;[10] or "they are of no concern to us" etc., it is nevertheless true that they are compelled towards the faith to which they are called, by divine grace alone.[11]

Again, turncoats such as these[12] are said, and rightly said, to prevaricate against Christ,[13] because having betrayed their own cause, i.e. by accepting the faith through baptism, they aid the other side through their infidelity

[6] *Cod.*, 1.7.5 [Who persuades a slave to abandon Christianity is to suffer capital punishment: "Eum quicumque servum seu ingenuum, invitum vel suasione plectenda, ex cultu Christianae religionis in nefandam sectam ritumve traduxerit, cum dispendio fortunarum capite puniendum censemus"].

[7] *Dig.*, 11.3.1.3 [Persuasion is more than compulsion and enforced obedience: "Persuadere autem est plus quam compelli atque cogi sibi parere"].

[8] x, 5.6.14 [To the archbishop of Sens and the bishop of Paris giving the right to try and punish a Jew who has struck a cleric. Although this was allowed to the ecclesiastic only in his role as a secular lord, the decretal would now provide the legal basis for trying Jews before church courts for what could be defined as ecclesiastical offences]; and x, 5.6.6 [excommunication for trafficking in contraband with Muslims; the gloss reads: "*Privatione*: hoc potuit papa facere contra laicos ratione criminis commissi"].

[9] [1 Cor. 5:12: "Quid enim mihi de iis qui foris sunt judicare?"]

[10] *Dig.*, 28.3.5. [Oldradus here refers to a complex and obscure discussion of the rights that a posthumous child, not specifically disinherited, has in an estate bequeathed to someone else on the basis of some condition. The text is to be found in the section dealing with the general subject of illegal, invalid, and broken wills. If he is trying to make some point about the disinheritance of the Jews as opposed to the newborn (Christians), he is certainly going about it in a roundabout way].

[11] Gratian, D.45.c.5 ["Sicut enim homo propria arbitrii voluntate serpenti obediens periit, sic vocante se gratia Dei propriae mentis conversione quisque credendo salvatur"]; with respect to which Innocent [IV] comments fully in his commentary on x, 3.34.8 ["Item licet non debeant infideles cogi ad fidem, quia omnes libero arbitrio relinquendi sunt, et sola Dei gratia in hac vocatione valeat, 45 dist. de Iudaeis ..."].

[12] [Now turning from the "harbourer" to his *protégé*.]

[13] Gratian, C.1 q.4 c.7 ["in prevaricantes in Christum ..."] and Gratian, C.2 q.7 c.24 ["nunc in Christi fide prevaricati sunt ..."]; Gratian, C.2 q.7 c.23 ["... qui suam et Christianam legem prevaricantur"].

and [Jewish] rite.[14] However, a prevaricator can be called to account before the judge in whose presence he has prevaricated and whom he has affronted by his prevarication, to be convicted by him and punished.[15] The Inquisitor is such a judge, deputized by the apostolic see to defend the faith. The same can be said of those who have collaborated in the crime.[16] Therefore, when the Jew of whom it is here asked [whether he can be tried by the Inquisition or not] oversteps his appointed limits, it is no wonder if he is overtopped by limits not his own.[17]

Item, one replies to the second and third articles with the arguments above;[18] for since in those matters falling within the limits of the

[14] *Dig.*, 47.15.1 [The prevaricator betrays first one side and then the other: "Praevaricator est quasi varicator, qui diversam partem adiuvat prodita causa sua. ... nam qui praevaricator, ex utraque parte constitit, quin immo ex altera"]; *Dig.*, 3.2.4.4 [Citing the same text].

[15] *Cod.*, 9.46.1 [Any calumny should be dealt with right away, while the case is being heard, and in the presence of the accuser: "Calumnia eo tempore coerceri solet, quo de causa praesente accusatore iudicatur"]; *Dig.*, 48.16.1.1 ["Calumniari est falsa crimina intendere, praevaricari vera crimina abscondere, tergiversari in universum ab accusatione desistere"]; *Cod.*, 2.7.1 [on the advocate's prevarication in court: "Si patronum causae praevaricatum putas et impleveris accusationem, non deerit adversus eum pro temeritate commissi sententia ..."; the gloss adds: "*Praevaricatum*: id est ex altera parte animo, et ex altera parte corpore, consistentem; item, si renunciet consilia suae partis"]; *Cod.*, 4.20.14 [Judges are to punish witnesses who are seen to be lying: "... data cunctis iudicibus absque ullo praescriptionis obstaculo (sicut saepe dictum est) testes, quorum voces falsitate vel fraude non carere perspexerint, pro qualitate videlicet delicti animadvertendi licentia." The gloss adds: "... testes (qui non erant de foro iudicis causae) qui inveniuntur incredibilia, an iudex eos posset punire, cum non sint de sua iurisdictione? dicitur quod sic; nec possunt allegare privilegium fori, quia dum sunt in iudicio debet cessare eorum privilegium"].

[16] As in *Sext.*, 5.2.13 cited above [p. 37, note 2].

[17] *Cod.*, 6.33.3 [The rights of an heir who can present a proper testament to a competent judge, where the *glossa ordinaria* notes: "*principalem*: ... unde cum suos terminos excedat exceditur a non suis terminis"]; and *Cod.*, 1.9.11 [unless they abstain from what is unlawful, respecting the use of the symbol of the cross during Purim, the Jews shall lose the religious privileges they have hitherto enjoyed: "Iudeos quodam festivitatis suae sollemni Aman ad poenae quondam recordationem incendere et sanctae crucis adsimulatam speciem in contemptu Christianae fidei sacrilega mente exurere provinciarium rectores prohibeant, ne locis suis fidei nostrae signum immisceant, sed ritus suos citra contemptum Christianae legis retineant, amissuri sine dubio permissa hactenus, nisi ab illicitis temperaverint"; where the gloss adds: "*temperaverint*: privilegium enim debet amittere, qui concessa sibi abutitur potestate"; an instance where a Christian emperor determines the nature of a Jewish festival].

[18] And also with *Cod.*, 1.9.8 [Jews living under Roman law will appear before Roman (= Christian) judges in matters governed by Jewish and Roman law: "Iudaei Romano communi iure viventes in his causis, quae tam ad superstitionem eorum quam ad forum et leges ac iura pertinent, adeant sollemni more iudicia omnesque Romanis legibus conferant et excipiant actiones"]; and for this, see *Cod.*, 1.10.1 [Jews have no right to possess Christian slaves; circumcising non-Jewish servants will bring capital punishment: "Iudaeus

[Inquisitor's] office he acts on behalf of the pope,[19] he will exercise his jurisdiction over anyone who violates his territory in order to make off with a catholic and drive him into the ways of error.[20]

Item, one replies to the fourth article with the argument of the gloss on the decretal *Sicut dignum*,[21] also expressed in the *Decretum* beginning at the text *illud vero fidentissime* etc.[22]

Item, one replies to the fifth article by reference to the second response in the law *Qui servo* in the section of the *Digest* entitled "On Theft,"[23] and

---

servum Christianum nec comparare debebit nec largitatis vel alio quocumque titulo consequatur. Quod si aliquis Iudaeorum mancipium vel Christianum habuerit vel sectae alterius seu nationis crediderit ex quacumque causa possidendum et id circumciderit, non solum mancipii damno multetur, verum etiam capitali sententia puniatur, ipso servo pro praemio libertate donando"; the gloss adds: "*capitali*: id est, perpetuo exilio"].

[19] As in *Dig.*, 1.16.7-8 [The proconsul of a province has greater authority than anyone else, after the emperor himself]; *Cod.*, 1.38.1 [as representative of the emperor the Vicar takes precedence over all others]; *Sext.*, 1.6.36 [the papal legate within the territory of his legation ranks above all others after the pope himself].

[20] *Dig.*, 1.19.3 [Imperial officers, even though they do not have the right of deportation, are authorized to keep out trouble-makers: "Curatores Caesaris ius deportandi non habent ... . Si tamen quasi tumultuosum vel iniuriosum adversus colonos Caesaris prohibuerunt in praedia Caesariana accedere, abstinere debebit ..."]. And as for these matters, Gratian, D.54 c.13 [respecting Christian maidservants of Jews, thus exposed to possible union with Jewish men: "Mancipia christiana, quecumque Iudeum conparasse patuerit, ad libertatem iuxta legum precepta sine ambiguitate perducite, ne, quod absit, religio Christiana Iudeis subiecta polluatur"]; and Gratian, *De Cons.*, D.4 c.94: [converts to Christianity are not to be allowed to return to Judaism; their children are to be taken from them if they have them circumcised: "Plerique ex Iudeis, qui dudum ad Christianam fidem promoti sunt, nunc blasphemantes Christum non solum Iudaicos ritus perpetrasse noscuntur, sed etiam abhominandas circumcisiones exercere. De quibus ... hoc sanctum decrevit concilium (Toledo, 633) ut huiusmodi transgressores ... ad cultum Christianae dignitatis revocentur .... Eos autem quos circumciderunt, si filii eorum sunt, a parentum consortio separentur." For Duns Scotus on taking Jewish children from their parents, cf. Edward A. Synan, *The Popes and the Jews in the Middle Ages* (New York, 1965), pp. 48, 180].

[21] x, 5.12.6 [They are not immune from the charge of homicide who helped the slayers of Thomas Becket and did nothing to stop the evil deed; the gloss adds: "Arg. ... dicit quod illi qui venerunt animo occidendi, feriendi aut capiendi illum sanctum virum, tamen manus non iniecerunt in illum, si de captione illa mors subsecuta fuisset, pari paenitentia vel fere pari sunt puniendi cum occisoribus." So any kind of sympathetic support that might frustrate the Inquisitor makes one as guilty as the principal offender].

[22] Gratian, C.4 q.6 c.1 [Those who falsely accuse bishops cannot henceforth give evidence in any ecclesiastical or criminal case: "... cum agere ceperit in episcoporum iudicio, si fuerit accusatoris persona dampnabilis, de cetero ad arguendum non admittatur, nisi proprias causas, non tamen ecclesiasticas vel criminales, asserere voluerit." Oldradus saw this as something to be used against those who hampered the work of the Inquisition].

[23] [*Qui servo* (*Dig.*, 47.2.36) held that whoever persuaded a slave to flee was not guilty of theft, unless he intended that someone else keep the slave, in which case he was party to the theft. But the second response (*Dig.*, 47.2.36.2) held that if a runaway slave took

to the paragraph beginning with *qui ferramenta* in the law *Si pignore*,[24] notwithstanding the first response to *Qui servo*,[25] because there a slave was persuaded to do what was allowed to him by natural law[26] and just as the slave was not liable, not even under natural law, so neither was the persuader.[27] In the case we are looking at now, however, the situation is quite the reverse and so [these laws] pose no obstacle.

Item, one replies to the sixth by the arguments above, and also [by reference to the Digest].[28]

To the seventh and last, one replies that although the matter in question causes injury to the Christian faith, and that therefore they ought to be compelled to stop by secular (and at least indirectly ecclesiastical) judges,[29] still, since no error is being introduced, the matter evidently does not belong to the office of the Inquisitor, whose function is limited.[30]

---

anything with him, the person who prompted him to run off was subject to an action for theft, as being an accomplice to the offender; this could be used against those Jews who encouraged their coreligionists to flee Crete.]

[24] *Dig.*, 47.2.55.4: ["Qui ferramenta sciens commodaverit ad effringendum ostium vel armarium, vel scalam sciens commodaverit ad ascendendum: licet nullum eius consilium principaliter ad furtum faciendum intervenerit, tamen furti actione tenetur." To lend tools or a ladder, knowing they will be used in a break-in, makes one liable to action for theft even if one has not counselled the crime. Just to help with the expenses of those fleeing Crete, without actually encouraging them to leave, is therefore actionable].

[25] *Dig.*, 47.2.36.1: [He is to be liable for theft who aids his son, slave or wife in the act of theft, even though they themselves may not be subject to action for theft. The implication is that slaves (= Jews) are not themselves subject to action for theft].

[26] As in *Dig.*, 15.1.9.7 [Slaves have natural rights; the slave who injures himself is not liable to his lord for damages, even though he is the lord's property, for natural law allows a slave to injure himself; "Si ipse servus sese vulneravit, non debet hoc damnum deducere, non magis quam si se occiderit vel praecipitaverit; licet enim etiam servis naturaliter in suum corpus saevire"].

[27] *Dig.*, 47.2.67.4 [To recommend a man as being suitable to lend money to and then substitute someone else in his place does not amount to theft unless the substitute actually knew of the substitution; in the case at issue, the persuader is not liable, since no offence has occurred: "Si tu Titium mihi commendaveris quasi idoneum, cui crederem, et ego in Titium inquisii, deinde tu alium adducas quasi Titium, furtum facies, quia Titium esse hunc credo, scilicet si et ille qui adducitur scit: quod si nesciat, non facies furtum, nec hic qui adduxit opem tulisse potest videri, cum furtum factum non sit"]; *Dig.*, 50.17.178 [following on the previous citation, if the principal case fails, so do all those that depend on it: "Cum principalis causa non consistat, plerumque ne ea quidem quae sequuntur locum habent"].

[28] *Dig.*, 48.9.6 [Those privy to a crime are to be punished as having committed the crime]; *Dig.*, 48.9.7 [The creditor who knowingly lends money to someone to purchase the commission of a crime is as guilty of the crime committed as the borrower].

[29] *Cod.*, 1.9.11 [above, p. 39, note 17].

[30] As in *Sext.*, 5.2.8.§4 [It is not the function of the Inquisition to investigate sorcery or divination unless there is some clear question of heresy: "Pestis inquisitores haereticae, a sede apostolica deputati, de divinationibus aut sortilegiis, nisi haeresim saperent manifeste,

Consilium 51

A Jew went over to the sect of the Saracens. The question is put, should he be punished?

Evidently not, since we tolerate both sects.[31] If each is in a state of damnation it does not matter to which sect he belongs because there is no distinction between equivalents,[32] and because whenever a matter is outside the church it is of no concern to us, according to the apostle who says metaphorically "what have we to do with those who are outside."[33] Neither Jews nor Saracens are bound by canonical constitutions.[34] For since God creates us with freedom of choice,[35] no one is forced into even the Catholic faith, which worships the truth and in which salvation is to be found completely;[36] all the less, therefore, is one compelled to Jewish superstition. However, once one has entered the Catholic faith one is compelled to preserve that faith intact,[37] for having once known the truth one ought not to turn back again, according to the word of Truth, who says

---

intromittere se non debent, nec punire talia exercentes, sed eos relinquere suis judicibus puniendos"].

[31] *Cod.*, 1.11.6 [Jews and pagans living peacefully are not to be attacked by Christians: "Christianis, qui vel vere sunt vel esse dicuntur, specialiter demandamus, ut Iudaeis ac paganis in quiete degentibus nihilque temptantibus turbulentum legisbusque contrarium non audeant manus inferre religionis auctoritate abusi"]; x, 5.6.13 [Christian piety accepts Jews whose guilt has placed them in perpetual servitude: "Etsi Iudaeos, quos propria culpa submisit perpetuae servituti ... pietas Christiana receptet ..."].

[32] For argument, *Cod.*, 1.3.54. [It is difficult to discern in this omnibus text dealing with a variety of matters what legal principle Oldradus has in mind. It may be the equivalence of Jews, pagans and heretics in the statement that no Jew, pagan or heretic may own Christian slaves: "nullus Iudaeus vel paganus vel haereticus servos Christianos habeat"; or it may be equivalence established by the removal of the inequitable treatment of a wife's property rights when both husband and wife enter religious life.]

[33] In 1 Cor. 5[:12], as adapted in Gratian, C.2 q.1 c.18.

[34] x, 4.19.8 ["... qui constitutionibus canonicis non arctantur ..."; the gloss adds: "*constitutionibus*: quae non arctant nisi illos qui subsunt ecclesiae directe; sed indirecte bene compelluntur"; though not bound by canon law directly, infidels may well be controlled indirectly. The decretal referred only to Muslims; Oldradus here applies it to Jews].

[35] Gratian, *De poen.*, D.2 c.40 §4 ["Liberi arbitrii nos condidit Deus ..."].

[36] Gratian, D.45 c.5 [Jews are not to be forced to accept Christianity: "De Iudeis autem precepit sancta sinodus (Toledo, 633), nemini deinceps vim ad credendum inferre"].

[37] As in the chapter cited, Gratian, D.45 c.5 [Those forced to adopt Christianity should be compelled to maintain the faith which they were forced into: "Qui autem iampridem ad Christianitatem coacti sunt ... quia iam constat eos sacramentis divinis associatos, et baptismi gratiam suscepisse, et crismate unctos esse, et corporis Domini extitisse participes, oportet, ut fidem, quam vi vel necessitate susceperint, tenere cogantur ..."].

in Luke 9[:62] "who puts his hand to the plough and looks back is not fit for the kingdom of God."[38] And of such it is said that it would have been better not to know the way of the Lord than, having known it, to turn back.[39] Such are said to "apostatize," that is, turn back.[40]

But this cannot be said of a Jew going over to the Saracen sect; since he did not know the truth, he evidently neither looked back nor departed from the way of the Lord—quite the contrary, since the Saracen sect is not as bad as that of the Jews, according to the word of the Lord, who says in Matthew 11[:24], "it shall be more tolerable for Sodom on the day of Judgement than for you." The prophet Ezekiel[41] tells them "you will justify Sodom," which Augustine explains as "in comparison with you Sodom is justified." And he says that the Jews are worse than the gentiles.[42] One ought not to be punished, therefore, for choosing the path of lesser evil.[43] The church makes sufficiently clear that they [Jews] are worse, for when it prays on Good Friday for all people there is no genuflection for Jews, although there is for pagans.[44]

Therefore they always recite laws punishing apostates when a Catholic passes to another sect.[45] If someone has undertaken to enter the Catholic faith and then changes to another, he is punished by exile, and so suffers a lesser punishment than if he were fully a Christian.

From the above it may be concluded that one is not punished for passing to another sect provided one has not entered the Catholic faith first.

[38] x, 3.34.7 ["... cum sit scriptum in evangelio 'Nemo mittens manum suam ad aratrum, et respiciens retro, aptus est regno Dei'"].

[39] x, 5.9.4 ["... quum minus malum existat viam Domini non agnoscere, quam post agnitam retroire"].

[40] Gratian, C.26 q.7 c.16 ["... sciant ... se fidem Christianam et baptismum prevaricasse, ... et apostatam, id est retro abeuntem et Dei inimicum, iram Dei ... incurrisse ..."].

[41] [16:51.]

[42] Gratian, C.1 q.1 c.37, and the reason is there noted [in the gloss: "*Peiores*: quia illi (gentiles) tantum naturalem legem transgressi sunt; Iudaei etiam scriptam. Illi praedicatores non habuerunt; isti etiam Iesum Christum. Apud illos nulla miracula sunt; apud istos multa facta sunt; et praeterea isti Christum crucifixerunt"].

[43] *Dig.*, 50.17.200 ["Quotiens nihil sine captione investigare potest, eligendum est quod minimum habeat iniquitatis"].

[44] [In the *Orationes sollemnes* on Good Friday.]

[45] *Cod.*, 1.9.16 [Jews who circumcise Christians are to be punished by confiscation of goods and exile]; and *Cod.*, 1.6.2 [those performing second baptisms are to suffer the death penalty]; *Cod.*, 1.6.3 [permission is not to be given to apostates to rebaptize; the punishment is exile].

CONSILIUM 71

May a Christian, without sinning, use the help or assistance of infidels in his own defence? It seems that he can, for what anyone does in defence of his body is considered to have been done as a matter of right,[46] especially if he cannot otherwise protect himself,[47] or has a reasonable fear that he cannot.[48] That is why one is pardoned not only if, in peril of his life, he should kill his attacker but also if he should kill someone else, even someone who is not of his attacker's company.[49] One cannot be blamed for wanting to save one's own skin.[50] Not only can we make war upon our enemies [in alliance] with infidels and deceivers, but we can use deceit in doing so.[51] After all, we put up with dogs in church to keep peace in the

[46] *Dig.*, 1.1.3 ["Nam iure hoc evenit, ut quod quisque ob tutelam corporis sui fecerit, iure fecisse existimetur ..."].

[47] *Dig.*, 9.2.45.4 ["Qui, cum aliter tueri se non possent, damni culpam dederint, innoxii sunt; vim enim vi defendere omnes leges omniaque iura permittunt"].

[48] *Dig.*, 9.2.49 [When one acts on the basis of a justifiable fear–in this case, of a threatening fire–then one is not required to make compensation for destroying neighbouring buildings].

[49] *Cod.*, 9.16.2, and the gloss there [If in fear of one's life, one is not held to blame for killing an attacker or anyone else: *Alium:* "qui cum agressore sit socius, vel, ut puto, etiam non socius, cum dicat in discrimine eum constitutum"]; argument in *Dig.*, 9.2.29.3 [where the damages were unavoidable, there is no action]; and *Dig.*, 47.9.3.7 [if in defending ourselves damage is unavoidably caused, there is no injustice done]; argument in *Dig.*, 38.2.14.6 [one should be pardoned, and not excluded from his succession, for desiring to punish a former slave in the face of deep provocation: "Si libertus maiestatis patroni filium accusavit et patroni filius calumniae eum capitis puniri desideravit, non debet repelli hoc edicto (concerning the property of freedmen). Idem puto et si ab eo petitus retorsit in eum crimina: ignoscendum enim est ei, si voluit se ulcisci provocatus"; the gloss adds: "*retorsit*: quasi socium criminis: ut sic repellatur ab accusando ... et no. ignoscendum ei qui non facit sponte"].

[50] *Dig.*, 48.21.1 [In cases carrying the death penalty it is no offence to corrupt an opponent–you cannot blame someone who does whatever he can to save his own life].

[51] Gratian, C.22 q.2 c.21 [As did the king of Israel: "Utilem simulationem et in tempore assumendam, Iesu regis Israel nos doceat exemplum, qui, cum non potuisset interficere sacerdotes Baal, nisi finxisset se ydolum velle colere, dicens 'Congregate michi omnes sacerdotes Baal. Achab servivit ei in paucis, ego serviam sibi in multis'"]; and Gratian, C.23 q.2 c.2 ["Cum autem iustum bellum susceperit, utrum aperte pugnet, an ex insidiis, nichil ad iusticiam interest"]; *Dig.*, 49.15.26 [it matters not whether a captive is released or escapes by force or guile: "Nihil interest quomodo captivus reversus est, utrum dimissus an vi vel fallacia potestatem hostium evaserit ..."].

church,[52] following the example of the Lord, who sometimes uses the wicked to administer his punishment.[53]

On the one hand, we find that in a just war the faithful obey and assist infidels;[54] that we use mathematics to keep track of our incomes[55] although the art of mathematics is prohibited in both testaments;[56] that Paul called himself a Pharisee in order to incite the Pharisees to his defence,[57] and sought soldiers from the praetor by whose aid he might avoid being harmed;[58] that the Maccabees, who were holy men and warriors for the faith, entered into an agreement with the Romans for mutual assistance[59] although the Romans were pagan; that Abraham allied himself with Eschol, went with him into war, yet he was not of his law;[60] that in time of necessity we communicate with the excommunicated; and that Solomon accepted wood from unbelievers for the construction of his temple.[61]

On the other hand, that verse of *Chronicles* 19 seems to stand in contradiction: "You help the ungodly, and you are joined in friendship with them that hate the Lord"; also, the king of Jerusalem was censured by the prophet because he wished to avail himself of the aid of the kings of Israel.[62]

But one replies to the first [objection] that the war was not a just war; and to the second, that the Israelites wanted to draw the people of Judah

[52] Gratian, C.23 q.4 c.18 [Some evils are to be punished, others must be tolerated].

[53] Gratian *post* C.23 q.5 c.49 ["Hinc notandum est, quod aliquando punit Deus peccata per nescientes, aliquando per scientes"].

[54] Gratian, C.11 q.3 c.94 ["Iulianus imperator, quamvis esset apostata, habuit tamen sub se Christianos milites ..."]; Gratian, C.23 q.1 c.44 ["Ordo autem naturalis mortalium paci accomodatus hoc pascit, ut suscipiendi belli auctoritas atque consilium penes principes sit"].

[55] *Cod.*, 9.18.4 [Those who use magic to plot against the lives of others, or to arouse sexual appetites, are to be punished; but not those whose purpose is innocent].

[56] [Being a form of necromancy.]

[57] Acts 23[:6].

[58] Gratian, C.23 q.3 c.1, dictum Gratiani ["Hinc de Paulo legitur quod ... petiit milites a pretore ..."]; Gratian, C.23 q.3 c.2 ["Neque enim apostolus Paulus vitae suae transitoriae, sed ecclesiae Dei consuluit, quando contra illos, qui eum occidere conspiraverant, consilium illorum ut tribuno proderetur effecit. Unde factum est, ut eum ad locum, quo fuerat perducendus, deduceret miles armatus, ne illorum pateret insidiis"].

[59] [1 Mach 8:17ff.]

[60] Gen 14[:13] and Mach 5 c. [Unidentified; perhaps this should read 1 Mach 10, where Jonathan makes a treaty with Alexander].

[61] [3 Kings 5.]

[62] 2 Chron 19[:2]; 2 Chron 20[:35-37]; Gratian, C.23 q.3 c.1 & 2 [see note 58] & 3.

and Jerusalem to worship golden calves.[63] Quarrels and strife should be sown amongst the wicked, for (as St. Gregory says in his *Moralia*) it is just as harmful when the virtuous are disunited as it is pernicious when the wicked are not.[64] Unity strengthens the perverse by bringing them together, for they are all the more incorrigible when of one mind. That is why Paul called himself a Pharisee, causing division between Pharisees and Sadducees, and there followed his liberation,[65] at which point the [biblical] gloss says that just as the unity of the righteous is beneficial, so the unity of the wicked is always harmful to the good.[66] Because of this, the Saviour in Luke 12[:51] says that he did not come to bring peace to the nations, but rather division, whence Isaiah [58:6]: "loose the bonds of wickedness, undo the bundles that oppress." Indeed, to procure discord among the enemy is the way of the wise general.[67]

[63] Gratian, C.23 q.3 c.1 and 2 [above, p. 45, note 58], and D.23 c.1 [This last is the electoral decree *In nomine domini* issued by Nicholas II in 1059, which has no bearing here. Possibly Oldradus' reference to *distinctio* 23 is an error of transcription for *causa* 23, which deals with questions of the just war].

[64] [Gregory, *Moralia in Iob* 33.31, *S. Gregorii Magni Moralia in Iob*, ed. Mark Adraen, 3 vols. Corpus christianorum, series latina, 143–143B (Turnhout, 1979–1985), 143B:1721.]

[65] Acts 23[:6].

[66] [*Bibliorum sacrorum cum glossa ordinaria ... et postilla Nicolae Lyrani ... tomus sextus* (Paris, 1590), col. 1219-1220; the comment is Bede's.]

[67] Which is what Vegetius means in his *de re milit.* in chapter 10 [cf. *Flavi Vegeti Renati epitoma rei militaris* 3.10, ed. Carl Lang (Leipzig, 1885), p. 92: "Inter hostes discordiarum serere causas sapientis est ducis. Nulla enim quamvis minima natio potest ab adversariis perdeleri, nisi propriis simultatibus se ipsa consumserit"], and on this see Isidore [*Sententia* 3.32 (PL 83:703)].

CONSILIUM 72

Whether a war against the Saracens of Spain is licit.

It is evident that those wishing to live in peace and quiet ought not to be disturbed[68] for the reason noted by Innocent, that no one should be forced into the faith.[69] And so it seems that war can be undertaken only against persecutors.[70]

And also for the reason that the Apostle gave the Romans: "henceforth your wars are not to be carried on in the flesh."[71] And Malachy 1[:11] says: "From the rising of the sun to its setting my name is great among the gentiles, and I am sanctified in every place, and there is offered to my name

[68] *Cod.*, 1.11.6 [Jews and pagans living peacefully are not to be attacked by Christians; see above, p. 42, note 31].

[69] Innocent IV, commenting on X, 3.34.8 ["Item licet non debeant infideles cogi ad fidem, quia omnes libero arbitrio relinquendi sunt, et sola Dei gratia in hac vocatione valeat"]; X, 5.6.9 ["Statuimus ut nullus Christianus invitos vel nolentes Iudeos ad baptismum venire compellat. Si quis autem ad Christianos causa fidei confugerit, postquam voluntas eius fuerit patefacta, Christianus absque calumnia efficiatur; quippe Christi fidem habere non creditur, qui ad Christianorum baptismum non spontaneus, sed invitus cogitur pervenire"]; Gratian, C.23 q.5 c.33 ["Ad fidem nullus est cogendus"]; Gratian, D.45 c.5 ["De Iudeis autem precepit sancta sinodus (Toledo 633), nemini deinceps vim ad credendum inferre"]; Gratian, D.45 c.3 [they should be persuaded with kindness, not aspersions: "Qui sincera intentione extraneos a Christiana religione ad fidem cupiunt rectam adducere, blandimentis debent, non asperitatibus studere, ne quorum mentem reddita a plano ratio poterat provocare, pellat procul adversitas"]; Gratian, C.23 q.4 c.53 [love one's neighbour as one's self: "Debet homo diligere proximum tamquam se ipsum, ut quem potuerit hominem beneficientiae consolatione, vel informatione doctrinae, vel disciplinae cohercione, adducat ad colendum"].

[70] Gratian, C.23 q.8 c.11 [The case of Jews is quite different from that of Saracens: "Dispar nimirum est Iudeorum et Sarracenorum causa. In illos enim, qui Christianos persecuntur, et ex urbibus et propriis sedibus pellunt, iuste pugnatur; hii ubique servire parati sunt"; the gloss adds: "Videtur ergo quod si Sarraceni non persequuntur Christianos, non possumus impetere eos. Nam etiam ad mensam eorum commedere possumus ... et lex dicit quod eis quiete degentibus nullam debemus facere molestiam"].

[71] Gratian, C.23 q.1 c.1 ["Quomodo enim eis bellorum proficeret ista descriptio ... quibus per Apostolum jubetur et dicitur (1 Cor:6): "non vosmetipsos vindicantes, sed magis injuriam percipite, et magis fraudem patimini?" Unde denique sciens Apostolus iam nobis ultra bella non esse carnaliter peragenda, sed animae certamina contra spiritales adversarios desudanda ..."]; and note the comment of the Archdeacon [= Guido de Baysio, who explains the Pauline text as meaning that war against the pagans was not necessary, since pagans no longer injured Christians: "Apostolus sciens vobis iam ultra bella non esse carnaliter peragenda scilicet contra paganos quia christianam religionem non lacerant. Antiquiis autem temporibus licebat bella indicere eis etiam quos sibi infestos non cognoscebant esse"; the conclusion being that warfare against the Saracens "carnaliter" might be renewed when provocation arises].

a clean oblation"; and for the reason in the chronicle of Ptolemy, in the prologue;[72] and also because of this: "You will constitute them princes over all the land.[73] Nor was their power narrow or limited but wide and full. And he reigned from sun up to sun down,[74] and from sea to sea, and from the water to the ends of the earth."[75] And for this: "The son whom he constituted the inheritor of the worlds";[76] on which [consult] Odo in the Christmas sermon, folio 15, where kings sin in taking tribute from them as payment for giving them peace, and at folio 20, that for possibly 600 years east and west had served Christ up to the time of Muhammad.[77]

But that it is legitimate to war against the Saracens [of Spain] is proven thus: Either because they attack Christians, and then there is no doubt,[78] for it is legitimate to meet force with force because what anyone does to defend oneself is considered to have been done by right;[79] or else they do not attack Christians, to which I say that war ought to be waged against them because it is quite likely that whenever they have the chance they will attack and oppress Christians and the Church, for this seems to be in their nature. Whence the Master states in his *Scholastic History*[80] that what is written in Genesis 16 regarding their father Ishmael from whom they descend[81] (namely that his hand is against all men, and the hand of all is against him, and he shall pitch his tents apart from all his brethren) is borne out by the Saracens who descend from his line, for they war against all men, and all war against them. Therefore although they may now be at peace, perhaps because they see no way of doing injury, they should be given no

[72] [L. Muratori, *Rerum italicarum scriptores* 2 (Milan, 1727), col. 755.]

[73] [Ps 44:17.]

[74] [Mal 1:11.]

[75] [Zach 9:12.]

[76] [Hebr 1:2.]

[77] [Possibly Odo of Chateauroux? For his Christmas sermons, see Johann Baptist Schneyer, *Repertorium der lateinischen Sermones des Mittelalters für die Zeit von 1150-1350* (Beiträge zur Geschichte der Philosophie und Theologie des Mittelalters, ed. M. Schmaus, bd. 43, heft 4, Münster, 1972), pp. 398-399, nos. 49-57.]

[78] As in Gratian, C.23 q.8 c.11 [above, p. 47, note 70].

[79] *Dig.*, 1.1.3 [above, p. 44, note 46]; *Dig.*, 9.2.45 [above, p. 44, note 47]; x, 5.39.3 [If a cleric repels force with force, he is not to be sent to the papal court for trial, citing the civil law "... quum vim vi repellere omnes leges omniaque iura permittant"].

[80] [Peter Comestor, *Historia scholastica*, Genesis, c. 49, "De fuga et ortu Ishmaelis," PL 198:1096.]

[81] As in the gloss on x, 5.6.13 ["*Ancillae*: id est Agar: quae significat synagogam. *Libera*, id est Sarra, quae significat ecclesiam. De Agar ancilla Sarrae descenderunt isti qui debent esse servi illorum qui descenderunt a Sarra, in quibus ecclesia fundata est"].

concession, since it seems likely that in the future they will disrupt the peace.[82]

Even supposing that now and in the future they might desire total peace, I still say that it remains a just and legitimate war. The entire province of Spain once belonged to Christians: there were churches there, and monasteries, and other holy places where Christ was praised and worshipped. These were under the Holy Catholic Church. The Saracens violently seized them, despoiling us by divine permission on account of our sins.[83] Although the greater part has now been recovered,[84] nevertheless they still hold a part. When we undertake to recover the homeland of which we were violently despoiled, such a war is legitimate,[85] and should be thought of as a defensive rather than an offensive war,[86] because whatever one does in self defence is considered to have been done by right, as in the law cited above.[87] Indeed this is what Innocent held,[88] that where territory

[82] Gratian, C.23 q.1 c.3 [War in this world is necessary to achieve the peace of the next; we use violence against the warlike (i.e. Saracens), and show mercy to the captive (i.e. Jews), especially where there is no threat to peace and order: "Si autem pax humana tam dulcis est pro temporali salute mortalium, quanto dulcior est pax divina pro eterna salute angelorum? Itaque hostem pugnantem necessitas deprimat, non voluntas. Sicut bellanti et resistenti violentia redditur, ita victoriis capto misericordia iam debetur, maxime in quo pacis perturbatio non timetur"].

[83] Gratian, D.56 c.10 [The Saracens as agents of God's retribution: "... donec iudex talium criminum ultrices penas per ignorantiam legis Dei, et per Sarracenos, venire et sevire permisit"].

[84] As in the gloss on Gratian, D.63 c.22 ["Obstat quod reges Hispaniae cum non subessent imperio, regnum ab hostium faucibus eruerunt"].

[85] As in Gratian, C.23 q.8 c.11 [above, p. 47, note 70].

[86] For arg. *Cod.*, 8.4.1 [One can use force to defend oneself against violence which threatens one's lawful possession: "Recte possidenti ad defendendam possessionem, quam sine vitio tenebat, inculpatae tutelae moderatione illatam vim propulsare licet"; where the gloss reads: "Si aliquis vult expellere me de fundo meo, quem recte possidebam, an possim ei resistere quaeritur. Respon. quod sic cum moderamine .... Item circa illud quod dixi de moderamine, primo quaeritur: quid si pugnus unius plusquam alterius ensis percutis. Respon. defendat se ense propter inaequalitatem virium, cum vim vi repellere omnia iura proclament"].

[87] *Dig.*, 1.1.3 [above, p. 44, note 46].

[88] In his comment on X, 3.34.8 [s.v. *Pro defensione:* "Quod autem Papa facit indulgentias illis, qui vadunt ad recuperandam terram sanctam, licet eam possideant Sarraceni, et etiam indicere bellum, et dare indulgentias illis, qui occupant terram sanctam, quam infideles illicite possident, hoc totum est ex causa. Nam iuste motus est Papa, si intendit terram sanctam, quae consecrata est nativitate, habitatione, et morte Iesu Christi, et in qua non colitur Christus sed Machometus, revocare ut incolatur, a Christianis. Item terra sancta iusto bello victa fuit ab Imperatore Romano post mortem Christi, unde licitum est Papae ratione Imperii Romani, quid obtinet illud ad suam iurisdictionem revocare, quia iniuste expoliatus est, et ab eo qui non habuit ius spoliandi eum, et haec ratio sufficit in omnibus aliis terris, in quibus Imperatores romani iurisdictionem habuerunt, licet posset dici

was at any time Christian, warfare [to regain it] is licit.

He has spoken more specifically on the matter, holding that jurisdiction and dominion can today belong to infidels.[89] However, Hostiensis holds the opposite view. And, saving the Truth, it seems that Hostiensis' opinion is closer to the truth, for Innocent's point [about lands that once belonged to Christians] clearly applies to all lands now held by the Saracens, for there is no place where the name of Christ has not been praised and worshipped. So we read of the Apostles that "their sound has gone forth unto all the earth and their words unto the ends of the world."[90] And the Saviour himself said to his disciples "You shall be my witnesses in all Judea and Samaria and to the ends of the earth."[91] Of Christ it is verified that all the kings of the earth will adore him and all people serve him.[92] Therefore Hostiensis says that nowadays infidels have no jurisdiction or dominion or honour or power. On the coming of Christ these were transferred to Christians, for the kingdom had been transferred from one people to another on account of its injustices.[93] All are subject to Christ, the sheep, the oxen and the cattle of the field, as Psalm 8 has it;[94] the gloss says that this means everything since it excludes neither heaven nor earth.[95] By sheep we mean Christians whose shepherd in the world the Saviour so describes himself, and he was the good shepherd because he gave his life

---

quod hoc iure scilicet ratione imperii non possit, cum ecclesia non habeat imperium, nisi in occidentem, 96 di. constan. Sed si non potest facere tanquam imperator, potest facere ex aliis praedictis causis, vel ad minus imperator potest facere, ut rex Hierusalem, ad quem regnum illud de iure venit, sicut credimus et credere debemus, ex quo contrarium nobis non constat, sed et contra alios infideles, qui nunc tenent terram, in quam iurisdictionem habuerunt Christiani principes, potest Papa iuste facere praeceptum et constitutionem, quod non molestent Christianos iniuste, qui subsunt eorum iurisdictioni, imo quod plus est, potest eos eximere a iurisdictione eorum, et dominio in totum"; *Innocentii quarti pontificis maximi in quinque libros decretalium* (Frankfurt, 1570); cf. Walter Ullmann, *Medieval Papalism: The Political Theories of the Medieval Canonists* (London, 1949), chapter 5 *passim*].

[89] [Commenting on x, 3.34.8: "... scilicet dominia, possessiones, et iurisdictiones licite sine peccato possunt esse apud infideles, haec enim non tantum pro fideli sed pro omni rationabili creatura facta sunt ...".]

[90] Gratian, D.19 c.7 [Citing Ps 18:5].

[91] Gratian, C.11 q.3 c.84 [Citing Acts 1:8]; and on this see Gratian, D.21 c.2 ["Ceteri ... apostoli ... qui etiam, iubente Domino, in toto orbe dispersi evangelium praedicaverunt"].

[92] Gratian, C.23 q.4 c.38 [Citing Ps 71:11].

[93] Gratian, C.23 q.7 c.2 [Citing St. Augustine: "... et ipsi Iudei, a quibus ablatum est regnum secundum verba Domini, et datum est genti facienti iusticiam ..."].

[94] Ps 8[:8].

[95] For the argument, see Gratian, D.19 [Gratian *post* D.19 c.1: "*Dicendo vero*: 'omnia decretalia constituta,' nullam de decretalibus constitutis pretermisit ..."; the gloss adds: "*Dicendo*: Arg. quod verbo generali omnia debent comprehendi"].

for his sheep.[96] Also, he committed them to Peter and to Peter's successors, to be nourished, to be instructed, to be increased.[97] But by oxen and cattle of the field we mean Saracens who, like beasts deprived of all reason, desert the true God and worship idols.[98] Saracens are called beasts literally, because their father Ishmael was called Onager by the Lord. The reason was, as Methodius says, because it was foreordained that his descendants would surpass all the savagery of beasts and the number of the meek would be ground down by them; for, he says, in sacred places they will slaughter priests, and in the same places will lie with women, and tether their animals at the tombs of the saints—all this because of the sins of Christians. These things the Master tells us in his *Historia Scholastica* in the aforesaid chapter on the flight of Hagar.[99] And indeed they have vented all this fury in the province [of Spain] with God's permission.[100]

And although these beasts do not appear to have been committed to Peter for feeding, nevertheless they have been placed beneath his feet[101] with respect to lordship and power. So we are to understand the Church in Abraham's words to his wife Sarah, who was complaining about that accursed handmaiden who despised her: "Behold," he says, "your handmaiden is in your own hand; use her as you wish";[102] for Sarah signifies the Holy Catholic Church, the handmaiden Hagar, the accursed sect of Muhammad which took its origins from her.[103] Therefore, the Holy Church, symbolized by Sarah, may use that accursed handmaiden as the

[96] [Corr. Jo 10:11]; Gratian, C.23 q.4 c.12 [referring to the same gospel].

[97] Gratian, C.8 q.1 c.9 ["Simon Iohannis amas me? Pasce oves meas"].

[98] And see "frumento" [This is probably Papias, *Elementarium doctrinae rudimentum* (rudimento = frumento?)] at the word *Saracenis* ["Sarrhaceni dicti quia ex sarrha se predicent genitos, vel sicut gentiles aiunt: quod ex origine Syrorum sunt quas syrigine: hi per amplam habitant solitudinem, ipsi cedar [sic] a filio ismahelis"; *Papias vocabulista* (*Vocabularum* [Venice, 1496; anastatic rpt. Turin, 1966). Papias got this from Isidore, *Etymologies*, 9.2.57].

[99] [Above, p. 48, note 80.]

[100] Gratian, C.7 q.1 c.47 [About Norman depredations, where the gloss adds: "*Divinitus*: Deus propter peccata hominum mittit flagella et persecutiones"].

[101] [Cf. Ps 8:8: "Omnia subiectis sub pedibus eius."]

[102] [Gen 16:6.]

[103] Gratian, C.23 q.4 c.39 [The church may chastise heretics as Sarah chastised Hagar]; Gratian, C.23 q.4 c.42 [citing Augustine; see below, p. 64, note 181: "... quam ecclesiam significabat Sara, quando persecutionem faciebat ancillae. Liberam quippe matrem vestram, celestem Ierusalem, id est veram Dei ecclesiam, in illa muliere dicit figuratam, que affligebat ancillam. Si autem melius discutiamus, magis illa persequebatur Saram superbiendo, quam Sara cohercendo. Illa enim faciebat dominae iniuriam, ista inponebat superbae disciplinam"].

blessed Sarah had used her, by beating her.[104] She may use her as her Lord commands, by driving her out and depriving her children of inheritance and possession, that they not share with the free children.[105] For since they are the offspring of a slave woman, and are therefore themselves slaves (for the children follow the womb)[106]—indeed, slaves reproved by the Lord[107]—they are not legally competent to hold rights of jurisdiction, lordship, or honour.[108]

Thus there can be no doubt that the war is licit, since it is directed to the defence of the faith, to the recovery of that land of which we were despoiled and in which Christ was worshipped, and to the increase, therefore, of the faith and the expulsion of that accursed handmaiden and her offspring. For this reason Holy Church and our preachers have always approved that war, by urging and encouraging kings to its undertaking, and applying to it many spiritual and temporal benefits, with good reason, because it is evident that the general council rightly equated the Spanish with the Jerusalem war.[109]

This is confirmed by the fact that tithes are assigned for such a pious act, since the common good is thus achieved—the good of clergy, of laity, of churches. It is therefore not unfitting that they share in the burden.[110] Likewise because consecrated and holy things ought to be sold to redeem

[104] As in Gratian aforesaid, C.23 q.4 c.42.

[105] Gratian, C.32 q.4 c.2 [Citing "Eiice ancillam et filium eius," Gen 21:10]; Gratian, C.32 q.4 c.3 [Abraham was not guilty of adultery when he had a child by Hagar]; Gratian, C.32 q.4 c.9 [after citing Gen 21:10: "Si igitur ancillae filius heres non est, nec ergo filius est"; so the offspring of Hagar, i.e. the Saracens, may be disinherited].

[106] *Dig.*, 1.5.5 [One is a slave if one's mother was a slave: "... iure gentium servi nostri sunt qui ex ancillis nostris nascuntur"].

[107] x, 5.6.13: "servi a domino reprobati"; [and above, p. 42, note 31].

[108] *Dig.*, 5.1.12 [Slaves do not perform public office: "... moribus feminae et servi (impediuntur), non quia non habent iudicium, sed quia receptum est, ut civilibus officiis non fungantur"]; et de arbit. l. parvi. § sed si servum [this reference seems to be in error; perhaps it is meant to refer to *Dig.*, 4.8.7: "Labeo writes in his seventh book that a slave cannot act as an arbiter"]; and *Dig.*, 41.1.19 [What a free man acquires, while acting as a slave, belongs to his master: "Liber homo, qui bona fide mihi servit, id quod ex operis suis aut ex re mea pararet, ad me pertinere sine dubio Aristo ait ..."].

[109] Gratian, C.23 q.8 c.32 [Second Lateran Council, respecting penance imposed on incendiaries; whether they go to Jerusalem or Spain makes no difference: "Penitencia autem ei detur, ut Iherosolimis aut in Hispania in servicio Dei per annum integrum permaneat"]; and note what the Archdeacon has to say on Gratian, C.23 q.7 c.2 [see below, note 117].

[110] *Dig.*, 14.2.2 [According to the Rhodian Sea Law, it is only fair that the loss occasioned by jettisoning some of the cargo to save the ship should be shared by those whose baggage was saved: "aequissimum enim est commune detrimentum fieri eorum, qui propter amissas res aliorum consecuti sunt, ut merces suas salvas haberent"].

captives.[111] This is done, moreover, that captives might be ransomed as well as the occupied churches which [the Saracens] hold, and that others might be protected, regarding which the sooner something is done the better.[112]

[111] *Cod.*, 1.2.21.2 [Sacred vessels may not be taken, sold, or melted down except where it is a question of redeeming captives: "Nam si necessitas fuerit in redemptione captivorum, tunc et venditionem praefatarum rerum divinarum et hypothecam et pignorationem fieri concedimus, cum non absurdum est animas hominum quibuscumque causis (in medieval texts, "vasis") vel vestimentis praeferri"]; Gratian, C.12 q.1 c.16: "... culpa est inminente ... necessitate res maxime desolatae ecclesiae captivis suis preponere, et in redemptione eorum cessare"; Gratian, C.12 q.2 c.70: "Aurum ecclesia habet, non ut servet, sed ut eroget et subveniat in necessitatibus"].

[112] *Cod.*, 2.40.5 ["Melius etenim est, intacta eorum iura servari, quam post causam vulneratam remedium quaerere"].

CONSILIUM 87

The question is put whether a prince can, without sin, expel Jews and Saracens from his kingdom and confiscate their goods; and whether the pope can order or urge princes to do so.

First, it seems not. For one ought not to disturb Jews living peacefully under one's rule nor confiscate their goods,[113] for they possess rights of lordship and ownership[114] to the extent that they can even receive revenues from Christians,[115] and they may acquire against Christians by prescription.[116] If the goods they hold have been justly acquired these ought not to be taken from them.[117] If a prince take their goods without cause he sins, because although he may be their lord in the sense of protector, nevertheless he is not to despoil them unjustly.[118] The reason is

[113] *Cod.*, 1.9.14 [Jews are not to be disparaged, exposed to contumely, nor their synagogues or dwellings burned]; *Cod.*, 1.11.6 [Jews and pagans living peacefully are not to be attacked by Christians; see above, p. 42, note 31]; x, 5.6.9 [see above, p. 47, note 69]; and x, 5.6.3 ["Sicut legalis diffinitio Iudaeos novas non patitur erigere synagogas, ita eos sine inquietudine veteres habere permittet"].

[114] *Cod.*, 1.9.9: ["Nemo exterus religionis Iudaeorum Iudaeis pretia statuet, cum venalia proponentur iustum est enim sua cuique committere"].

[115] x, 5.6.2 [The Christian slaves of Jews are to be freed, but if they continue to work the land of their former lords, they must continue to make the customary payments].

[116] The gloss on *Porro* in Gratian, C.16 q.3 c.14 [Where violence is in question, there is no prescription of time; "Secus si mansueti sunt Iudaei vel Sarraceni, tales bene praescriberent ..."].

[117] As in the gloss on Gratian, C.23 q.7 c.2 ["Dicunt quidam quod Iudaeis et Sarracenis licite possum sua auferre, et intelligunt id quod dicitur i.q.viii. c.dispar (above, p. 47, note 70) de personis Iudaeorum, non de rebus. Sed secus credo, quia Iudaei solvunt tributum et de voluntate nostra tenent ea quae habent"]; on which point see the Archdeacon [= Guido de Baysio, who cites the thirteenth-century canonist Laurentius Hispanus: Jews should not be despoiled of their possessions. We may despoil Saracens inasmuch as they hold our land; but where they are willing to surrender it peacefully, we should not injure them any more than the Jews. Guido also reports Laurentius as being of the opinion that Christians should not attack Saracens holding territory that never belonged to Christians. He adds that there is a difference between Jews, whom we ought not to injure or to despoil, and "pagans or Saracens," whom we should, and cites *dispar*, above, p. 47, note 70].

[118] As in the gloss on *Cod.*, 7.37.3 [On the security of title of those who have obtained goods or lands from the public treasury; the gloss notes: "Si aliquis emebat a fisco statim securus erat"]; and Innocent [IV] on x, 3.49.8, [a discussion of ill-gotten gains; near the end he deals with the case of secular law "contra ius naturale, puta quod dominia de uno in alium transferrentur sine causa"]. Innocent says, as does Hostiensis in commenting on x, 3.34.8, that the pope ought not to confiscate their goods; rather he ought to tolerate them; Gratian, D.45 c.3 ["Qui sincera intentione extraneos a Christiana religione ad fidem cupiunt rectam adducere, blandimentis debent, non asperitatibus studere ..."]; and x, 5.6.13 ["Etsi Iudaeos, quos propria culpa submisit perpetuae servituti ... pietas Christiani receptet ..."].

that we may be able to gain them for God through our life in common with them.[119] Jews are especially to be tolerated because they are useful to our faith. Whence Augustine says, commenting on Psalm 40: "The Jews serve us like the slaves who carry our books, for they keep clean of error the books we study—the books, that is, in which are the Law and the Prophets by which Christ is foretold. By their books we demonstrate [the truth of] our faith to pagans and other unbelievers; for when [the pagans] hold our own books suspect we convince them all the better with the books of our enemies [the Jews]."[120] Gregory in his homily on John says that at the end of the world they will be enlightened by Christ.[121] If they were driven from the face of the earth none would remain, although the law says that the remnants of Israel shall then be saved. And that they ought to be tolerated is proved by what Augustine says in his comment on Psalm 40 where he says that they were prefigured by Cain who slew his brother and therefore received a mark that he not be killed; so that this perverse people is marked, not to be slain, but rather to be tolerated.[122]

But although a private person may not trouble them, it seems that a prince can, especially the Jews, because they were made slaves through the death of Christ,[123] and this judgement was executed by Constantine;[124] hence the Archdeacon [Guido de Baysio] says[125] that the prince, who is their lord, can sell them; therefore all the more can he expel them.[126] And

[119] Gratian, C.23 q.4 c.17 ["Infideles non possumus Christo lucrari, si colloquium eorum vitamus et convivium"]; and the argument on Gratian, C.11 q.3 c.24 [John Chrysostom, who refers to pagans only, not Jews: "Ad mensam quippe paganorum si volueris ire, sine ulla prohibitione permittimus"; where the gloss adds: "*Permittimus*: Ad hoc ut eos lucremur"]; and see x, 4.19.7.

[120] [In Ps 40.14: "modo, fratres, nobis serviunt Iudaei, tamquam capsarii nostri sunt, studentibus nobis codices portant"; *Sancti Aurelii Augustini enarrationes in Psalmos* (Corpus christianorum, series latina, 38; Turnhout, 1956), p. 459.]

[121] [PL 76:1176: "Notandum, fratres, est quod in fine mundi ad Redemptoris fidem etiam Judaea colligetur ... ."]

[122] [Ibid.]

[123] x, 5.6.13 [above, p. 42, note 31].

[124] As Hostiensis notes in commenting on x, 5.6.7 [stipulating that Jews are not to build new synagogues, but may repair old ones: "Constantinus Imperator tulit libertatem ecclesiis, et iudaeos servituti subiecit ... nam de iure hoc operata est mors Christi"].

[125] On Gratian, D.45 c.3 [cited above, p. 47, note 69: "Credo quod principes quorum sunt servi iudei possunt eis auferre filios parvulos absque omni iniuria, cum illi in filiis non habeant potestatem tanquam servi ... idem principes possent eos parvulos tanquam mancipia sua aliis dare vel vendere in servitutem invitis parentibus"].

[126] For the argument, see *Cod.*, 4.55.1&2 [The sale of slaves on condition that they are sent out of the country; if they later obtain their freedom they can be reduced to slavery again if found in those places forbidden to them].

it is for that very reason, the Archdeacon says,[127] that the prince can confiscate their goods, since they hold these merely as a *peculium* [what a lord might give a slave]; for this [conclusion] he adduces the *Decretals* where it says that if [Jews] are converted [to Christianity] their goods are not to be confiscated;[128] therefore, [arguing] from the contrary sense, if they are not converted, they can. There is better support in the same section of the *Decretals* where it says that they are not to be disturbed nor deprived of their goods without licence of the territorial power;[129] with such licence, therefore, they can be. Furthermore, they are tolerated out of piety and as a matter of grace.[130] [Their toleration] ought not therefore to be ascribed to necessity;[131] if one is cared for, through even the slightest efforts of a friend, that is sufficient.[132] They have nothing to complain about, since they have received the grace of alien status, as Boethius says in his book *De consolatione*.[133] This seems to be true where danger or scandal threatens Christians.[134] For when they abuse our grace the ungrateful deserve to lose their privilege.[135] This becomes clear in the case of churches that are burdened because Jews do not pay tithes on their possessions. Therefore lords who possessed land ought to have been compelled to rent their fields

[127] In his comment on Gratian, D.54 c.15 [on converts to Christianity: "*Percipiant*: dicunt quidam quod iudei istud pretium et res suas cum sint servi non possident ut proprias, sed ut pecu-lium. Unde per dominum suum eis possunt privari ad libitum, nisi cum ad fidem convertantur ..."].

[128] x, 5.6.5 ["... a possessionibus suis nullatenus excludantur, quum melioris conditionis ad fidem conversos esse oportet, quam, antequam fidem susceperint, habebantur"].

[129] x, 5.6.9 ["Nullus etiam Christianus eorum (Judeorum) quemlibet sine iudicio terrenae potestatis vel occidere vel vulnerare vel suas ... pecunias auferre praesumat, aut bonas, quas hactenus ... habuerunt, consuetudines immutare, praesertim in festivitatum suarum celebratione quisquam fustibus vel lapidibus eos nullatenus perturbet"].

[130] As it says in the chapter "Etsi Iudaeos" [x, 5.6.13 above, p. 42, note 31].

[131] *Dig.*, 1.16.6 [Rules about a proconsol's acceptance of gifts. It would be coarse to refuse everything offered, no matter what, but contemptible to seek something from every-one, and sheer greed to snatch everything possible. Moreover, token gifts must not be piled up so as to amount to a substantial gift that is unnecessary. So, too, the Jew will have to be satisfied with token toleration].

[132] *Cod.*, 2.18.20 ["Tutori vel curatori similis non habetur, qui citra mandatum negotium alienum sponte gerit ... ac satis abunde sufficit, si cui vel in paucis amici labore consulatur"].

[133] [*De cons. phil.* 2, pr. 2; ed. E.K. Rand, rev. S.J. Tester, Loeb Classical Library (Cambridge, Mass., 1973), p. 180, ll. 14-16: "Habes gratiam velut usus alienis, non habes ius querelae tamquam prorsus tua perdideris."]

[134] As noted by Innocent [IV] in his commentary on x, 3.34.8 ["Imo si male tractarent Christianos, posset eos privare per sententiam iurisdictione et dominio, quod super eos habent, tamen magna causa debet esse, quod ad hoc veniat, debet enim Papa eos quantum potest sustinere, dummodo periculum non sit Christianis, nec grave scandalum generetur"].

[135] As in the chapter "Etsi Iudaeos" [x, 5.6.13, above, p. 42, note 31].

to such as would pay the tithes.[136] All this seems clearly prefigured in that slave woman [Hagar] from whom they descend since, because she conducted herself haughtily and ungratefully to the free woman [Sarah], who signifies the church, she was expelled. For it was said, "Expel the slave woman and her son."[137]

However, where they have been living quietly and there has been no scandal, it does not seem right that the pope should require or urge princes [to expel them], for the reason noted in the *Decretal* "Quod super his,"[138] and because they are not his concern, being outsiders.[139]

Moreover, Gregory [I] seems in his register to have warned and ordered the prelates of Sardinia if they had pagan rustics to increase their assessments so that in consequence they might turn to the path of truth,[140] whereas in another letter, which he sent to the procurator of the

[136] X, 3.30.16 ["De terris ... quas Iudaei colunt, tuae prudentiae respondemus, ut eos ad decimas persolvendas, vel ad possessiones penitus renunciandas cum omni districtione compellas, ne forte occasione illa ecclesiae valeant suo iure fraudare"]; X, 5.19.18 ["Principibus autem iniungimus, ut propter hoc non sint Christianis infesti, sed potius a tanto gravamine (usury) studeant cohibere Iudaeos. Hac eadem poena Iudaeos decernimus compellendos ad satisfaciendum ecclesiis, pro decimis et oblationibus debitis, quas a Christianis de domibus et possessionibus aliis percipere consueverant, antequam ad Iudaeos quocumque titulo devenissent, ut sic ecclesiae conserventur indemnes." This might be compared with a form letter on the subject, contained in a formulary of the Audientia Litterarum Contradictarum at the time of Boniface VIII: "Conquestus est nobis ... rector ecclesie de ... quod B. et F. de ... Iudei in parrochia ipsius ecclesie habitantes decimas de proventibus domorum et possessionum, que a Christianis in eadem parrochia devenerunt ad ipsos, prout a Christianis antea solvebantur, eidem ecclesie solvere indebite contradicunt in eiusdem ecclesie preiudicium et gravamen.—mandamus, quatinus, si est ita, dictos Iudeos ad debitam satisfactionem decimarum huiusmodi monitione premissa per subtractionem communionis fidelium appellatione remota previa ratione compellas"; Peter Herde, *Audientia litterarum contradictarum* (Tübingen, 1970), 2:283 (K. 133); cf. ibid., 1:345].

[137] Gratian, C.23 q.4 c.41 [The text "Eiice ancillam" etc. is from Gen 21:10].

[138] X, 3.34.8.

[139] X, 4.19.8 [Citing 1 Cor 5:12: "quid enim ad nos, secundum Apostolum ... de his qui foris sunt iudicare"].

[140] Part of that letter is in Gratian, C.23 q.6 c.4 ["... si rusticus tantae perfidiae et obstinationis fuerit intentus, ut ad Dominum minime venire consentiat, tanto pensionis onere gravandus est, ut ipsa exactionis suae pena conpellatur ad rectitudinem festinare." Cf. *S.Gregorii Magni registrum epistularum* ed. Dag Norberg, Corpus christianorum, series latina, 140 (Turnhout, 1982) 4:26 (p. 245)].

patrimony, he seems to speak differently when referring to Jews, since he does not say that they may not have Jews and that [the procurator] may increase their assessments, but rather that he is to promise them remission of their payments, that they might thus be converted the more swiftly.[141]

[141] [Ibid 2:50 (p. 141): "Quia autem multi Iudaeorum in massis ecclesiae commanent, volo ut, si qui de eis Christiani voluerint fieri, aliquantum eis pensio relaxetur, quatenus isto beneficio provocati, tali desiderio et alii assurgant."]

Consilium 91

The question has arisen whether Saracens should be forced to pay tithes for lands in their possession, and how they should be compelled. It is in favour of the Saracens that they have never paid the tithe, and that those lands have always belonged to Saracens.[142]

I believe that they are required [to pay]. Since tithes are [a form of] tribute,[143] they have to be paid by any sort of proprietor,[144] even by an infidel.[145] Since therefore He is the Lord of all, as it says in the Psalms: "The earth is the Lord's and the fullness thereof,"[146] all who till the earth must pay the tithe to Him.[147] Indeed, a lord who possesses land is to be compelled by ecclesiastical censure to give out his land for cultivation to those who pay the tithe to churches without making trouble,[148] which appears sufficiently to be the intent of the law, especially according to Innocent [III] who uses the Saracens as an example.

[142] For this last point there is support in x, 5.19.18 [Jews must continue to pay tithes for lands acquired from Christians which the previous owners had paid, so that the churches not lose their incomes], and so from the contrary etc. [In other words, if lands acquired from Christians owe tithes, lands not acquired from Christians do not].

[143] Gratian, C.16 q.1 c.66 [Paying the tithe is also good for the health: "Decimae tributa sunt egentium animarum. Quod si decimam dederis, non solum habundantiam fructuum recipies, sed etiam sanitatem corporis consequeris"].

[144] x, 3.30.28 ["... circa res acquisitas vel factas de pecunia decimata, quum ipsae venduntur, credamus deducendas expensas, et de residuo quasi de lucro decimas persolvendas, ut, si vendatur domus, ager, vinea, clibanus, molendinum, grex aut quaelibet merces" etc.]; *Cod.*, 4.47.2 and 3 [establishing the liability to pay taxes of those who bought land under condition of not paying taxes on it].

[145] x, 3.30.16 [Land held by Jews is subject to the tithe: "De terris quas Iudaei colunt ... respondemus ut eos ad decimas persolvendas, vel ad possessiones penitus renunciandas cum omni districtione compellas, ne forte occasione illa ecclesiae valeant suo iure fraudari"]; x, 3.30.26 [All are to pay the tithe, without discounting seed and other expenses first].

[146] As cited in x, 3.30.26.

[147] Proof in *Cod.*, 10.16.1 [Who possesses the land must pay the tribute: "... annonas ... is solvere debet qui possessiones tenet et fructus percipit"].

[148] x, 3.30.32 [Citing the Fourth Lateran Council: "... ut ipsi domini, talibus personis et taliter sua praedia excolenda committant, quod absque contradictione ecclesiis decimas cum integritate persolvant, et ad id, si necesse fuerit, per censuram ecclesiasticam compellantur"].

Notwithstanding the custom in predial tithes.[149] Notwithstanding that they pay [tribute] to the king, for if what is owed to one is paid to another, [the debtor] is not thereby freed from his obligation;[150] tithes cannot pass to a layman;[151] rather, the king appears to commit sacrilege in receiving the tithe.[152]

Notwithstanding what is said about the land always belonging to Saracens, because it is not true; in fact everything around the [Mediterranean] sea was once Christian, and so when recovered should return to its former state;[153] even assuming that it had not belonged to Christians, nonetheless from the time it fell under the lordship of Christ it ought to be ruled by divine law, that law by which tithes have been established.[154] It cannot be denied that the land now belongs to Christians and that the Saracens are only labourers or *coloni*.

149 As in x, 3.30.32 [This refers to the practice, mentioned by Oldradus, of giving out lands to erstwhile non-Christians in order to avoid paying the tithe: "His nonnulli domini praediorum ea tribuunt excolenda, ut decimis defraudentes ecclesias, maiores inde reditus assequantur"] and commented on fully by Johannes Andreae in his rubric on *Sext.* 3.13.2. [On the *decimae novalium* see Lorenzo Simeone, "Novali," in *Encyclopedia cattolica*, 8, 1968–1969].

150 *Cod.*, 8.42.12 ["Invito vel ignorante creditore qui solvit alii, non se liberat obligatione"]; x, 2.24.22 ["... ut intelligas per te ipsum quod onus non remittitur set augetur, quum cuiquam improvide solvitur quod alii ex debito est praestandum"].

151 As in x, 2.24.22; and x, 3.30.17 [Church tithes or oblations cannot be conceded to the laity].

152 Gratian, C.16 q.7 c.1 [Laymen must not possess tithes: "Decimas ... possideri a laicis apostolica auctoritate prohibemus. Sive enim ab episcopis vel regibus vel quibuslibet personis eas acceperint, nisi ecclesiae reddiderint, sciant, se sacrilegii crimen conmittere ..."]; and x, 3.30.25 [No royal exception can exempt one from paying the tithe: "Porro cum laicis nulla sit de spiritualibus concedendi vel disponendi attributa facultas, imperialis concessio, quantumcunque generaliter fiat, neminem potest a solutione decimarum eximere, quae divina constitutione debentur"].

153 *Dig.*, 11.7.36 [When a place, which ceases to be sacred when captured by the enemy, is recovered, it is restored to its former state: "Cum loca capta sunt ab hostibus, omnia desinunt religiosa vel sacra esse ... quod si ab hac calamitate fuerint liberata, ... reversa pristino statui restituuntur"]; Gratian, C.7 q.1 c.42 [Pope Gregory I appoints bishop John of Alessia as cardinal bishop of the church of Squillace in Calabria, a temporary measure while his own city is occupied by enemies; he should return to his prior charge if and when conditions allow. Cf. Stephan Kuttner, "Cardinalis: The History of a Canonical Concept," *Traditio* 3 (1945) 133].

154 As in x, 3.30.14 ["Quum decimae non ab homine, sed ab ipso Domino sint institutae, quasi debitum exigi possunt"].

Notwithstanding the contrary argument[155] because it would introduce a contrariety of law and offend against the gloss on the law "Conventiculam" in the *Codex.*[156]

As for the second [question], about how they are to be compelled: one can first say, in the way described in the decretal cited above,[157] namely that lords who possess lands may be compelled not to give them lands to work; and second, according to the decretal *postulasti.*[158]

[155] Which might be drawn from x, 5.19.18 [Jews are to compensate churches for the tithes which Christians, previous owners of their homes and lands, should have paid. One might therefore conclude by the argument *a contrario sensu*–improperly–that because they are not required to do so when the previous owner was Jewish, Jews are not ordinarily obliged to pay the tithe].

[156] *Cod.*, 1.3.15 [This forbids illicit religious gatherings outside churches. The gloss cites the principle: "Verbum quod non respicit finalem causam non induxit argumentum a contrario sensu." In other words, contrariety in law only has to do with its purpose or end. In this case, the fact that such gatherings are prohibited outside the church does not allow one to argue that they are permitted inside the church: "... quod licet extra ecclesiam prohibeat, non ideo in ecclesia permittit"].

[157] x, 3.30.32 [above, p. 59, note 148].

[158] x, 5.6.14 [above, p. 38, note 8].

Consilium 264

That opinion seems the sounder, namely that without a legitimate reason a prince cannot expel peaceful Jews, Saracens and other pagans from his lands.

First, because it is the necessary consequence of both natural and divine law that whatever a prince wishes to be justly done to himself he do to others, especially to his servants or tributaries,[159] and not do to others what he does not wish done to himself.[160] Now, he does not wish to be expelled from the kingdom. Therefore, let him not expel others from the kingdom. He is required, indeed, to love Jews and Saracens insofar as they share his nature, not only in soul but in body.[161] To expel them, then, without cause is clearly opposed to the precepts of charity. "The love of one's neighbour works no evil," neither of expulsion nor of any other wickedness;[162] charity does not act perversely;[163] and no upright will does what is wicked.[164] Such divine and natural law cannot be dispensed from because it cannot be changed,[165] not even by the pope, since its change necessarily involves sin[166]

[159] Matt 7[:12], Gratian, D.1 ["Humanum genus duobus regitur, naturali videlicet iure et moribus. Ius naturae est, quod in lege et evangelio continetur, quo quisque iubetur alii facere quod sibi vult fieri, et prohibetur alii inferre quod sibi nolit fieri. Unde Christus in evangelio: 'Omnia quecunque vultis ut faciant vobis homines, et vos eadem facite illis. Haec est enim lex et prophetae'"].

[160] x, 1.33.13 ["Quum igitur non deceat alii te fecisse quod ab alio fieri tibi nolles ..."].

[161] As it says in Gratian, *De Poen.*, D.2 c.5. §5 ["Non illi proximi nostri tantum credendi sunt, quos nobis gradus sanguinis iungit, sed proximi nostri credendi sunt omnes homines naturae nostrae ... participes"]; and in what follows, ibid. § 6, [where it says] when we think of their sins and perils, just as we hope to be aided in ours, so we help them; and further on, [where it says] therefore, beloved, act with such love that the good you wish for yourself you also wish for your neighbour.

[162] Rom 13[:10: "Delectio proximi malum non operatur"].

[163] 1 Cor 13[:4: "Charitas non agit perperam ..."].

[164] Gratian, *De Poen.*, D.2 c.5 ["Karitas est, ut michi videtur, recta voluntas, ab omnibus terrenis ac presentibus prorsus aversa, iuncta Deo inseparabiliter et unita, igne quodam Spiritus S. a quo est et ad quem refertur, incensa, inquinamenti omnis extranea ..." etc.].

[165] *Inst.*, 1.2.11 [The laws of nature cannot be changed: "Sed naturalia quidem iura, quae apud omnes gentes peraeque servantur, divina quadam providentia constituta, semper firma atque immutabilia permanent"]; Gratian, D.5 c.1 §1 ["Naturale ius inter omnia primatum obtinet et tempore et dignitate. Cepit enim ab exordio rationalis creaturae, nec variatur tempore, sed immutabile permanet"].

[166] Confirmed by the gloss on *Quedam* in x, 2.24.26 [If oaths are legitimate why does the pope forbid them? which is why the pope says, in this decretal: "Quaedam enim prohibentur quia per se mala, ut furtum, adulterium, et huiusmodi: quae non sunt aliquatenus facienda"].

and alters the goodness of nature, which is impossible.[167] Hence it is that according to the law of nature and out of love we must help them when in need, and give them alms.[168]

Second, mercy is due the captive enemy, especially where there is no fear that the peace will be disturbed; all the more so should such mercy be extended to a tributary slave, that he not be expelled.[169] Princes are required to show love to the respectful and the obedient, to do nothing from a wish to injure, but to do everything from loving care—to do nothing brutally or inhumanely.[170] Whatever [unpleasant] has to be done should be done not in anger but in love.[171]

Third, for the same reason that we ought not to despoil peaceful Jews, pagans and Saracens of their goods, we ought not to deprive them of home and birthplace.[172] What they possess, they possess by the law of nations, whether things or places, or else they possess by legal title, and so by right according to human, not divine justice,[173] as Innocent clearly holds.[174] And that they cannot be expelled, except they be persecutors, is well supported

[167] Gratian, D.13, §1 ["... adversus naturale ius nulla dispensatio admittitur ..."]; Gratian, D.1 c.1 ["Ius naturale est commune omnium nationum, eo quod ubique instinctu naturae, non constitutione aliqua habetur ..."].

[168] Gratian, D.42 c.2 ["Non enim ex vita eorum, quos accipis, mercedem tibi retributurus est Deus, sed ex voluntate et ex honorificentia multa, ex misericordia, et bonitate"]; Gratian, C.16 q.1 c.5 [Do not provide any more than is necessary: "Christianum, quem senseris tibi aut semper aut crebro de nummis loquentem, excepta elemosina, que indifferenter omnibus patet, institorem potius habeto quam monachum. Preter victum, et vestitum, et manifestas necessitates nichil cuiquam tribuas, ne filiorum panes canes comedant"]; Gratian, D.86 c.16 [to be a well wisher is not enough: "Non satis est bene velle, sed etiam bene facere"].

[169] Gratian, C.23 q.1 c.3 ["Sicut bellanti et resistenti violentia redditur, ita victoriis capto misericordia iam debetur, maxime in quo pacis perturbatio non timetur"].

[170] Gratian, C.23 q.5 c.4 ["Nichil nocendi cupiditate fiat, sed omnia consulendi karitate, et nichil fiat inmaniter, nichil inhumaniter"].

[171] Gratian, C.12 q.2 c.11 ["... ex karitate agendum est, et non ex furore, quia ipsi hoc prestatur, qui corrigitur, ne gehennae ignibus tradatur"].

[172] This is proved by the gloss on *Per hoc* in Gratian, C.23 q.7 c.2 [above, p. 54, note 117].

[173] Gratian, C.14 q.4 c.11 ["Hoc enim certe alienum non est, quod iure possidetur, hoc autem iure, quod iuste, et hoc iuste, quod bene"]; x, 5.40.12 ["Ius dictum est a iure possidendo. Hoc enim iure possidetur, quod iuste, hoc iuste, quod bene ..."].

[174] [Innocent IV] in his comment on x, 3.34.8; this is supported by Gratian, C.23 q.5 c.34, where it says "vindicavit iustissime" ["Si propterea persecutor non fuit Nabuchodonosor, quia scelus in sanctum Danielem commissum vindicavit iustissime; quomodo vindicandum est a regibus, quod Christi sacramenta exsufflantur, si Prophetae membra, quia in periculum missa sunt, sic vindicari meruerunt?" and the gloss concludes that heretics can be punished by kings].

according to the contrary alternative.[175] It is the property of innocence, especially that of kings, to bring injury down on no one.[176] Mildness and clemency is part of the Christian religion, cruelty certainly is not.[177]

Item, third,[178] Hagar, the mother of the Agarenes, and her son Ishmael,[179] father of the Agarenes, were expelled by Sarah[180] because she [Hagar] persecuted her mistress and he [Ishmael] his brother Isaac. Regarding each persecution Augustine speaks clearly.[181] Therefore where the Agarenes abide humbly and do not deceive simple Christians to follow the cult of their vile Muhammad they are not therefore to be expelled but are to be accepted.[182]

Item, fourth, pagans and Jews are to be counted among the sheep of Christ through creation, governance, and redemption on the part of Christ. Whence the Lord in the gospel of John 10[:16] says: "I have other sheep that are not of this sheepfold" meaning the Church. So the pope has power over them as over his own sheep which Christ committed to him

[175] Gratian, C.23 q.7 c.2 ["... qui ea terra male utebantur expulsi sunt"; and so, Oldradus suggests, if they do not, they should not be expelled].

[176] Gratian, C.23 q.5 c.37 ["Non est innocentiae parcendo sinere, ut in malo gravius incidatur. Pertinet ergo ad innocentis offitium non solum nemini malum inferre, verum etiam a peccato cohibere, vel punire peccatum, ut aut ipse, qui prius odio habetur, corrigatur experimento, aut alii terreantur exemplo"]; Gratian, C.6 q.1 c.14 ["Sapiens non est omnis qui nocet"].

[177] Gratian, C.23 q.5 c.3 ["Unum solum est, quod in tua iusticia pertimescimus, ne forte (quoniam quicquid mali contra Christianam societatem ab hominibus inpiis ingratisque conmittitur, profecto gravius est et atrocius, quam si in alios conmittatur) tu quoque pro inmanitate facinorum, ac non pocius pro lenitatis Christianae consideratione censeas cohercendum"].

[178] [Oldradus seems to have forgotten that a third point had already been made.]

[179] [Now turning to Muslims.]

[180] [Gen 16.]

[181] Gratian, C.23 q.4 c.42 [Cites Augustine; it is really the Muslims, signified by Hagar, who persecute the Christians, not the other way around: "Si ecclesia vera ipsa est, que persecutionem patitur, non que fecit, querant ab Apostolo (Gal 4:6), quam ecclesiam significabat Sara, quando persecutionem faciebat ancillae. Liberam quippe matrem vestram, celestem Ierusalem, id est veram Dei ecclesiam, in illa muliere dicit figuratam, que affligebat ancillam. Si autem melius discutiamus, magis illa persequebatur Saram superbiendo, quam Sara cohercendo. Illa enim faciebat dominae iniuriam, ista inponebat superbae disciplinam ..."]; and where proud Ishmael reared his head and sought to seduce his brother by playing with him, Gratian, C.32 q.4 c.2 [Citing Augustine on John, tract. 11], because he thought to have Isaac worship vile images which he had made, as the gloss says where it begins "Ishmael."

[182] Confirmed by Gratian, C.23 q.4 c.39, where the angel says to Hagar: "Revertere ad dominam tuam" [Gen 16:9].

along with other things in the last chapter of John [21:17], saying: "Feed my sheep," not distinguishing between these sheep and those.[183]

Since, therefore, the pope ought to feed them, by word and by example and with courtesy—provided that they are not rebels—he should not therefore attack them nor allow them to be injured.[184]

Fifth, infidels are to be led to the faith neither by terror nor harsh dealings, neither violence nor expulsion, but by kindness, by gifts, so that the whole shape of justice be preserved as well as freedom of choice.[185] Moreover, a man should love his neighbour as himself so that, as best he can, he may lead him to the worship of God through either helpful comfort, or doctrinal formation, or the straitness of discipline. If Jews were legally expelled everywhere, the words of Isaiah and Paul respecting them would fail, the words "their remnant shall be saved"[186] would not be fulfilled, and they would not be witness to our faith as established by Eusebius in book 3 of his *Ecclesiastical History*, chapter 7, putting it quite neatly: "On this account the Jewish people were driven from their kingdom for the crime of disbelief, and dispersed throughout the lands, their temple, their sacrifice and the kingdom itself destroyed, compelled to be witnesses everywhere to the faith of Him whose enemies they are, their name and race preserved in a few old sacraments, being scattered among the gentiles without distinction to bear witness to the truth, like Cain flying from the face of the Lord."[187] And Augustine in his Epiphany sermons: "Therefore He did not slay the Jews, that is He did not drive them from the face of the earth, lest they forget the law which by reading they remember, with the result that they might apply judgement to themselves, but to us might proffer witness for the Truth."[188]

183 X, 1.33.6 §6; and so Innocent [IV] holds in his comment on X, 3.34.8.

184 As it says in X, 4.10.1 ["Durum est enim, ut, si alii pro mercede libertates tribuunt, ab ecclesia, a qua tueri debent, revocentur"].

185 Gratian, D.45 c.3, which nicely confirms this [above, p. 47, note 68]; and Gratian, D.45 c.5 [above, pp. 42, 47, notes 36, 69]; and is best supported by Gratian, C.23 q.4 c.53 where it is put best of all, and where in fact the infidel is called "neighbour" [above, p. 47, note 69].

186 Rom 9.27 ["Si fuerit numerus filiorum Israel tanquam arena maris, reliquiae salvae fient" (Cf. Is 10:12)], which is noted in the gloss on the Gratian, C.28 q.1 c.11 ["*Iudaeorum*: quidam intelligunt hoc casus quod Iudaeis auferendi sunt parvuli eorum, et baptizandi, sed adulti nequaquam. Sed certe sicut nec adulti, ita nec parvuli ad fidem vi trahendi sunt; immo secundum hoc in brevi nullus est Iudaeus. Quomodo ergo reliquiae Israel salvae fierent postea?"].

187 [In fact, while Eusebius did describe the events in Jerusalem, following Josephus, these words come from Augustine's third epiphany sermon (PL 38:1032 sermo 201, c. 3).]

188 [Ibid.]

Sixth, the word of the Apostle supports this, teaching masters how they ought to treat their obedient servants in the last chapter of Ephesians:[189] "And you, masters, do the same to them," meaning servants, "forbearing threats, knowing that the Lord of both you and them is in heaven and that God is no respecter of persons." And at the beginning of the last chapter of Colossians:[190] "Masters, do unto your servants what is just and equitable, knowing that you too have a master in heaven."

Whence just as Saracens or other unbelievers living among us are to be punished for their crimes,[191] they are not to be expelled or punished without cause.[192]

Again, just as infidels are not to be expelled from their possessions, so these are not to be taken from them; just as, indeed, they are not to be expelled from their ancestral homes.[193] Just so, the sons of Israel did not expel the Jebusites from Jerusalem.[194]

[189] Last chapter [6:9].

[190] Last chapter, at the beginning [4:1].

[191] x, 5.17.4 [The king of Sicily committed to various bishops the judgement of Saracens who had kidnapped Christian women and children, and killed some. Alexander III allowed the ecclesiastical judges to impose fines, and even corporal punishment short of bloodshed. If, however, the matter called for death or mutilation, the decision was to be reserved to the royal court].

[192] Gratian, D.56 c.7 [One should be punished for one's own fault, not deprived because of the deception of others: "Satis perversum et contra ecclesiasticam probatur esse censuram, ut frustra quorundam, voluptatibus quis privetur, quem sua culpa vel facinus ab offitiis, quo fungitur, gradu non deicit"]; x, 1.2.2 [New constitutions are cast in the future tense so that no penalty is imposed on past acts made in ignorance of what would later be forbidden: "Rem quae culpa caret, in damnum vocari non convenit. Quoties verum novum quid statuitur, ita solet futuris formam imponere, ut dispendiis praeterita non commendet, ne detrimentum ante prohibitionem possint ignorantes incurrere, quod eos postmodum dignum est vetitos sustinere"; an argument against expulsion now for what occurred in the past].

[193] Gratian, D.26 c.3 [If someone who is married before baptism marries someone else after baptism, that is bigamy; the first spouse is not therefore to be expelled]; and also x, 5.6.5 at the part where it says "a possessionibus suis" etc. ["Si qui praeterea Deo inspirante ad fidem se converterint Christianam, a possessionibus suis nullatenus excludantur, quum melioris conditionis ad fidem conversos esse oporteat, quam, antequam fidem susceperint, habebantur"]; x, 5.6.9 [see above, p. 56, note 129]; x, 5.6.13 at the beginning where it says that Christian piety accepts and supports cohabitation with them, and therefore they are not expelled.

[194] Jud 1:21 ["Iebusaeum autem habitatorem Ierusalem non deleverunt filii Beniamin: habitavitque Iebusaeus cum filiis Beniamin in Ierusalem, usque in praesentem diem"]; Gratian, C.11 q.3 c.22 ["Audi ergo scripturam dicentem, quia non potuerunt filii Iuda disperdere Iebuseos, sed habitaverunt cum ipsis in Ierusalem usque in hodiernum diem"].

Seventh, there are specific examples in the *Codex*[195] where it is said that we ought not to molest those who conduct themselves peaceably, and in the gloss on the canon *dispar* in the *Decretum* at the point where it says "who persecute Christians";[196] so, in the contrary sense, if they do not persecute [Christians] they may not be injured or attacked.[197] Besides, it is written there[198] that "the heaven of heavens is the Lord's, but the earth he has given to the children of men"; therefore it is lawful for each to live anywhere, even the slave, provided only that he pay as tribute what he owes his lord by reason of his lordship.[199] Therefore what the law of human society grants should be denied to no one.[200]

Furthermore, the cause of the expulsion of the Amorites, Caananites and Jebusites from their lands by the children of Israel was their sins, especially idolatry which is against the law of nature that shouts out that God is one.[201] Jews and Saracens are not idolaters, although otherwise infidels; nor are they the public enemies of ruling Christian princes; therefore they ought not to be expelled.[202]

[195] *Cod.*, 1.11.6 [See above, p. 42, note 31].

[196] Gratian, C.23 q.8 c.11, where it says "qui Christianos persequuntur."

[197] So argues the gloss on this text [above, p. 47, note 70]; supported by Gratian, C.16 q.3 c.14 at the point where it says "where the fury of pagans and unbelievers" etc.; so in a contrary sense. And see the gloss at that point [above, p. 54, note 116].

[198] [Ps 113:6.]

[199] x, 3.39.2 ["Omnis anima sublimioribus potestatibus subdita sit; et vos subditi esse debetis. Ideo enim tributa praestatis, quia haec est probatio subiectionis"]; Gratian, C.11 q.1 c.28 ["Si enim censum Filius Dei solvit, quis tu tantus es, qui non putas esse solvendum?"].

[200] There is a good argument in Gratian, C.23 q.2 c.3 ["Notandum sane est, quemadmodum iusta bella gerebantur a filiis Israel contra Amorreos. Innoxius enim transitus negabatur, qui iure humanae societatis equissimo patere debebat"; where the gloss adds: "*Transitus*: Licet enim transire per alienum agrum ius non sit ... tamen quia necessarius et innoxius erat iste transitus isti prohiberi non debuerunt ... quia via publica erat et nemo prohibetur via publica uti"] and to the point is Gratian, D.5 c.4 ["Si ergo influxu sanguinis posita laudabiliter potuit Domini vestimentum tangere (Matt 9), cur, que menstruam patitur sanguinis, ei non liceat ecclesiam intrare? Si enim ea bene presumsit, que vestimentum Domini in languore posita tetigit, quod uni personae infirmanti conceditur, cur non con-cedatur cunctis mulieribus, que naturae suae vitio infirmantur?" where the gloss adds: "Arg. quod uni conceditur per consequens videtur aliis esse concessum ..."].

[201] Rom 1[:20] where it says "invisibilia Dei" etc.

[202] For argument see Gratian *post* C.23 q.5 c.49, Jos 5 and 7, Deut 7, and Gen 15; all of which may be sufficient for the canonist and mature theologian, but for [non-professional] people you will add subtle legal and canonical arguments. [This seems to be an aside to the person for whom Oldradus wrote the consilium].

CONSILIUM 333

In what way may a Jew be punished who has had carnal knowledge of a Christian woman? It must be acknowledged that the Jew cannot marry the Christian woman, because marriage is a communication sanctioned by divine law;[203] since such is not the case here it is clear that there is no marriage.[204] One who contracts such a marriage would be punished as an adulterer.[205] But with respect to any other kind of congress of Jew and Christian woman, aside from the fact that it is prohibited by the *Decretals* there is no explicit law saying that the man is to be punished as an adulterer.[206]

What if it be said in argument that, if such a union be subject to punishment when disguised as a marriage, as mentioned above, all the more should it be [subject to punishment] when not so disguised.[207] But this does not carry much weight. First, that in forming an illicit union [*commixtio*] one commits an illegality with respect to the sacrament of matrimony;[208] but it is quite the contrary if only a matter of sexual desire,[209] which is what I understand in this particular case, there being no other circumstances, such as abduction, rape, or incest, that would add to this

[203] *Dig.*, 23.2 ["Nuptiae sunt coniunctio maris et feminae et consortium omnis vitae, divini et humani iuris communicatio"]; *Cod.*, 9.32.4 ["Adversus uxorem, quae socia rei humanae atque divinae domus suscipitur ..."].

[204] Gratian, C.28 q.1 c.15 ["Cave, Christiane, gentili aut Iudeo filiam tuam tradere"].

[205] *Cod.*, 1.9.6 [The marriage of Jew and Christian is defined as adultery: "Ne quis Christianam mulierem in matrimonium Iudaeus accipiat neque Iudaeae Christianus coniugium sortiatur. Nam si quis aliquid huiusmodi admiserit, adulterii vicem commissi huius crimen obtinebit, libertate in accusandum publicis quoque vocibus relaxata"].

[206] [I.e., capital punishment, which in Roman law had long since ceased to mean death, although it might still be a very severe corporal penalty, as this case would prove.]

[207] *Dig.*, 48.5.39 ["Si adulterium cum incesto committatur, ut puta cum privigna nuru noverca, mulier similiter quoque punietur. Id enim remoto etiam adulterio eveniret." One is still punishable when the element of one of two crimes is removed. Presumably the same principle applies in the case under discussion: punishment is still deserved even if one leaves aside the offence of an illicit marriage].

[208] *Cod.*, 1.6.1 [Referring to another offence against a sacrament, that of rebaptism].

[209] *Nov.*, 39.2 [The woman who bore a child eleven months after the death of her husband, and so broke the law about remarrying within one year of widowhood, and might have lost her nuptial endowment as a consequence, excused herself on grounds of natural concupiscence: "Illa—sed quomodo dicamus verba illius erubescimus—non dignam se dicebat esse ut caderet, quia legem nosset de legitimis loquentem nuptiis ... porro partum hunc esse opus naturalis concupiscentiae"]; and *Novels* 74, *in prin.* [allowing for the automatic legitimization of the offspring of a union "puro affectu" if the couple later married. Both these cases illustrate a legal distinction between sexual union and marriage].

union some further offence; for then he might properly be punished more seriously because of the additional crime.[210] But these circumstances are not present in his accosting the woman.[211] Therefore he should not receive capital punishment as an adulterer.[212]

Nonetheless, I do not say that this foul union should not receive some kind of civil punishment at the discretion of a judge.[213] The fact that he was forced to confess and was not put to the question does not seem to be prejudicial to him, since he only confessed as to ordinary things, he had not confessed to any previous judgments, and [the confession] contravened the privilege granted to the Jews by Queen M., whereby what he said did nothing to instruct the court.[214]

However, let the Lord Judge consider that glory is not to be achieved by severity, but that in minor matters a judge ought to be inclined to mildness, while in graver he should apply the law with sympathy and temper its severity with mercy.

[210] *Cod.*, 9.13.1 [Who abducts a married woman is to be punished the more severely for having committed a double crime: "Quae multo magis contra eos obtinere sancimus, qui nuptas mulieres ausi sunt rapere, quia duplici crimine tenentur tam adulterii quam rapinae et oportet acerbius adulterii crimen ex hac adiectione puniri"].

[211] *Dig.*, 47.10.15.15 [The offence of accosting a woman is mitigated if she is improperly or misleadingly attired: "Si quis virgines appellasset, si tamen ancillari veste vestitas, minus peccare videtur: multo minus si meretricia veste feminae, non matrum familiarum vestitae fuissent."

[212] *Cod.*, 9.9.28(29) [As for the woman caught in adultery, it must be asked whether she owns an inn, or was only a servant there, or if she encouraged drunkenness, and so on; the gloss adds: "Seius commisit stuprum cum tabernaria: an possit accusari ob stuprum? Distinguitur, aut tabernaria erat domina tabernae, aut ministra, quae propinaverat vinum portantibus(sic); primo casu punitur, secundo non ... . *Quae adulterium*: id est stuprum, lex enim Iulia promiscue utitur hoc verbo"].

[213] *Dig.*, 47.18.1.1 [Where no penalty has been prescribed in the imperial rescripts, the punishment is left to the discretion of the person hearing the case: "Expilatores, qui sunt atrociores fures (hoc enim est expilatores) in opus publicum vel perpetuum vel temporarium dari solent, honestiores autem ordine ad tempus moveri vel fines patriae iuberi excedere. Quibus nulla specialis poena rescriptis principalibus inposita est: idcirco causa cognita liberum erit arbitrium statuendi ei qui cognoscit." Note also Oldradus' argument for a punishment *civiliter* rather than *capitaliter*].

[214] *Dig.*, 48.18.9 [Slaves are not to be "put to the question," e.g. to testify against their lords; even an interrogation without torture of such a slave is of no value: "Ex quibus causis quaestio de servis adversus dominos haberi non debet, ex his causis ne quidem interrogationem valere"] and note [the gloss to the effect that if the slave is not to be tortured, then his evidence is of no value: "*valere*: quasi dicat servus non debet torqueri, ergo tortus quod dixit non valet." Oldradus here finds support for disallowing evidence obtained by torture from Jews (= slaves)].

I, Oldradus, wrote the aforesaid and affixed my seal; but Lord R[aymond] of Apulia and Lord Anthony de Cruce, both of whom then occupied the office of judge in Avignon, condemned the said Jew, whose name was Pandonus, to be castrated. I saw the physical evidence of the excision before the palace.[215]

[215] [The royal palace which housed the secular court in Avignon, not the papal palace.]

THE LATIN TEXTS

A Note on the Latin Texts

The Latin texts of the consilia have been taken from *Oldradi de Ponte Laudensis ... Consilia, seu Responsa* (Frankfurt, 1576). Obvious errors have been corrected from Vatican MS Ross. 1096 and University of Kansas MS G.18. Such corrections are enclosed in brackets [ ]. Changes having to do with capital letters, paragraphs, punctuation, dittography, replacing the ampersand with et, ae with e, and the like have been made without comment.

CONSILIUM XXXVI

Infrascripti sunt articuli inquisitoris heretice pravitatis in partibus Romanie. In primis quidam Iudeus baptizatus et Christianus effectus longo tempore stetit in Christianismo. Postea negata fide Christi lapsus est in Iudaismum, quem quidam Iudeus suscepit in domo sua, sciens eum esse Christianum, et longo tempore secum tenuit, et uxorem Iudeam ei dedit, et sic eum fovit in iudaismo. Item quidam alius Iudeus emit unum puerum Christianum quem circuncidit et negare fidem Christi fecit, vocatis adhoc quibusdam aliis Iudeis qui una cum eo circunciderunt; et mortuo principali unus illorum qui in eius circuncisione fuerant dictum puerum suscepit et secum multo tempore tenuit, et tandem timens inquisitionem misit eum in Alexandriam ne posset reduci ad Christianismum. Item idem Iudeus emit unam Christianam et eam fecit iudaizare, negata fide Christi. Postea eam in uxorem duxit de qua suscepit duos filios. Et quia factum erat iam manifestum Christianis, eam veneno occidit. Mortuus est autem cum ea filius parvulus quem lactabat. Postea eo mortuo commissarii eius superstitem filium miserunt in Alexandriam ne posset per Christianos requiri tanquam filius Christiane. Item cum quidam Iudeus fuisset accusatus quod fuerat Christianus, et de hoc inquireret inquisitor, quidam alter Iudeus fecit pactum cum accusato pro certa summa pecunie, quod infra certum tempus eriperet eum de manibus inquisitoris qui eum tenebat sub fideiussione, et fecit quantum potuit, verbis, scriptis, et actis, clericos et laicos concitando contra inquisitorem, ita quod vix inquisitor potuit habere veritatem de heretico accusato. Item quidam Iudei baptizati in diversis partibus venerunt in insulam Crete et ibi vivebant ut Iudei. Et dum de talibus inquisitor inquireret, aliqui Iudei qui eos sciebant esse Christianos in tantum eos molestaverunt ut recederent de terra, ne possent per inquisitorem capi et reduci ad Christianismum, quod coacti sunt recedere receptis conductis et expensis ab illis Iudeis, quos tunc, cum scivit, inquisitor persecutus est, et quosdam cepit; alii vero fugerunt ad terras Sarracenorum. Item quidam Iudei emunt Christianos, et portant in Alexandriam, ubi vendunt eos Iudeis et Sarracenis, de quibus constat eis quod faciunt negare fidem Christi. Item aliqui Iudei in parasceve crucifigunt agnum sive ovem, et crucem conspuunt et pedibus conculcant in vituperium Iesu Christi. Nunc queritur qualiter potest procedi contra tales.

Ad primum articulum respondetur quod contra talem Iudeum poterit per inquisitorem procedi sicut receptatorem heretici, ut extra de here. c.

Contra christianos. Fuit enim talis receptator hereticus, ff. de recepta. l.1 et 2 et C. de his, Qui latro. vel alios crimin. reos occultant, l.1 et 2. Crimen enim receptationis committitur etiam ex uno actu, ar. ff. ad l.Iul. de adul. l.Mariti lenocinium § [Questum]; et colligi potest extra de pen. c. Felicis, li. 6; nedum hic, ubi fuit actus per tempus continuatus, ar. C. de inces. nup. l.Qui contra; et talis receptator non fuit sola receptatione contentus, sed per matrimonium cum Iudea eo procurante contractum. Videtur crimini iudaismi et apostasie que heresi equipollet favisse, imo ad ipsum plectenda suasione traxisse, ut C. de apos. eum, Quicunque. Et talis suasio plus est quam compulsio, ff. de servo cor. l.1 § Persuadere. Si autem Christianus hoc fecisset, constat quod contra eum procedi posset per inquisitorem. Sed nunquid excusabitur quia Iudeus? Dico quod non, quia ratione delicti fit de foro ecclesie, ut extra de Iudeis. c. Postulasti; et not. infra eo. tit. c. Ita quorum. Et si dicatur nihil ad nos de his [qui] foris sunt, verum est ut per [excommunicationem] possit cogi, quia cum excommunicatio eiiciat extra ecclesiam, in Iudeo locum non habet qui extra ecclesiam est, ut ff. de iniu. rup. et irri. te. l.Nam et si sub conditione. Vel nihil ad nos, etc. Verum est ut compellant[ur] ad fidem ad quam sola divina gratia vocantur, ut 45. distin. de Iudeis. Et de hoc plene notat Innocentius extra devo. et vo. red. c. Quod super. Item tales apostatantes dicuntur prevaricari in Christum, ut 1 quest. 4, Iudei, et 2 quest. 7, Non potest, et c. Alieni; et recte, quia [prodita] causa sua, id est, assumpta fide per baptismum diversam partem adiuvant per infidelitatem et ritum, ut ff. de prevaricatoribus l.1 et de his, qui not. inf[r]a l.Athleta § pen. Prevaricator autem potest coram iudice, coram quo prevaricatus est, et cui prevaricationis iniuriam irrogavit, accusari, convinci, et per eum puniri, ut C. de calum. l.1; ff. ad tur. l.1 § 1; C. de advo. di. iu. l.1; et de testi. l.Nullum. Et talis est iudex ad defensionem fidei per sedem apostolicam deputatus, sicut inquisitor. Et hoc idem contra cooperantes in crimine, preallegatum c. Contra christianos. Ideo cum Iudeus de quo queritur excesserit suos terminos, non est mirum si a non suis terminis excedatur, C. de edi. divi Adri. tol. l.ultim., et de Iudeis. l.Iudeos.

Item respondetur ad secundum et tertium articulum per superiores [rationes], et pro hoc C. de iu. l.Iudei; et C. ne mancip. Christian. here. vel paga. vel Iude. habeat. l.uni; cum enim, quantum ad ea que sunt de limitibus officii, fungatur vice Pape, ut ff. de off. proc. et le. l.Si vel in aliam, et l.seq.; C. de of. vic. prefe. l.1; extra de elec. c. Si abbatem; contra omnes suam iurisdictionem exercebit, qui ad predia sua tumultuosus accedit, ut de catholico furtum faciat et errare compellat, ut ff. de off. procur. cesa.

l.ultima. Et de his habetur 54 di. Mancipia; et de consec., dist. 4, Plerisque ex Iudeis.

Item respondetur ad 4 articulum. arg. extra de homi. c. Sicut dignum. Et videtur expressum 4 quest. 6 c.1 ibi illud vero fidentissime etc.

Item respondetur ad quintum articulum, ff. de furt. l.Qui servo [in secundo responso; et l.Si pignore § Qui ferramenta. Non obstat primum responsum eiusdem l.Qui servo;] quia ibi persuasum fuit contra servum quod sibi naturaliter licebat, ut ff. de pec. l.Sed si damnum § Si ipse. Et sicut contra ipsum servum etiam naturalis non fuit orta obligatio, ita nec contra persuasorem, ut in eo. tit. l.Sed si is, qui rem § Si tu Titium; et de reg. iur. l.1, Cum principale. In casu autem de quo queritur est totum contrarium et ideo non obviat.

Item respondetur ad sextum per superiores rationes, et pro hoc, ff. ad l.Pompeiam, de pari. l.Utrum, et l.Si sciente.

Ad septimum et ultimum respondetur quod licet istud de quo in questione contraria proponitur fiat in iniuriam fidei Christiane, et per hoc ut desistant debeant per ordinarios seculares et ecclesiasticos saltem indirecte coerceri, ut C. de Iudeis. l.Iudeos; quia tamen per hoc error non inducitur, non videtur quod spectet ad officium inquisitoris cuius officium est limitatum, ut extra de hereticis. c. Accusatus § Sane.

CONSILIUM LI

Iudeus transivit ad sectam Saracenorum. Queritur an sit puniendus. Et videtur quod non cum ambe iste secte tolerentur a nobis, ut C. de paganis l.Christianus; et extra de Iude. Et si Iudeos. Si utrobique sit in statu damnationis non est curandum in qua earum sit quia non refert quid ex equipollentibus fiat, arg. C. de epis. et cle. l.Deo nobis; et cum ubique sit extra ecclesiam nihil ad nos de eo iuxta verbum Apostoli dicentis 1 ad Corin. 5 c: 'Quid ad nos de his qui foris sunt?' transumptive positum, 2 q.1 Multi. Et Iudei et Saraceni constitutionibus canoni[ci]s non ligantur, extra de divor., Gaudemus. Nam cum liberi arbitrii creaverit nos Deus. de pe. di. 2, Si enim; etiam ad fidem catholicam, que veritatem colit, in qua perfecte salus invenitur, nemo compellitur, 45 dist. De Iudeis. Multo ergo minus quis ad superstitionem iudaicam compellitur, et omnino ad fidem catholicam semel susceptam servandam quis compellitur, ut d.c. De Iudeis; quia ex quo veritatem agnovit non debet amplius retro ire, iuxta verbum veritatis dicentis, Luce 9: 'Qui ponit manum ad aratrum et respicit retro non est aptus regno Dei', extra de voto, Magne. Et de tali dicitur quod melius fuisset viam domini non agnoscere quam post agnitam retro ire, extra de aposta. Quidam. Et tales dicuntur apostatare, id est retro abire, 26. q. fi. c. Observetis. Sed hoc de Iudeo ad sectam Saracenorum transeunte dici non potest, quia cum veritatem non agnoverit non videtur retro respicere nec viam domini relinquere. Imo cum secta Saracenorum sit minus mala quam Iudeorum, iuxta verbum domini dicentis Matthei 11: 'Tolerabilius erit Sodomis in die iudicii quam vobis'; Et Propheta Ezechiel dicit eis: 'Iustificatis Sodomam', quod exponens Augustinus: 'in cooperatione vestra iusta facta est'. Et dicit quod Iudei peiores sunt gentilibus, 1 q.1 Nonne; et que sit ratio ibi no. Non est ergo puniendus qui viam minus malam elegit, ff. de reg. iu. l.Quoties. Et quod sint peiores satis denotat ecclesia, quia cum in die parasceve oret pro omnibus, pro Iudeis non flectit genua, sed pro paganis sic. Et [ideo] leges punientes apostatas semper loquuntur quando catholicus transit ad aliam sectam, C. de Iude. Iudei. et ne sanctum baptis. reiteretur. l.2; imo hoc videtur probari in l.fi. Nam si aliquis initiavit fidem catholicam et convertit se ad aliam punitur pena exilii et sic minori quam si esset perfecte Christianus. Per que videtur sentire quod si non initiasset fidem catholicam licet transiret ad aliam non puniretur.

CONSILIUM LXXI

Nunquid Christianus possit sine peccato ad defensionem suam uti auxilio sive adiutorio infidelium? Et videtur quod sic. Nam quod quis ob tutelam sui corporis fecerit iure fecisse existimatur, ff. de iusti. et iur. l.Ut vim; maxime si se aliter tueri non potest, ff. ad l.Aquil. l.Scientiam § Qui cum aliter; vel si iuste timet quod se aliter tueri non possit, eod. tit. l.Si quis fumo. Inde est quod in periculo vite constituto ignoscitur, non solum si aggressorem occidat, sed etiam si alium etiam non socium, C. ad l.Cor. de sica. l.2; et l.Is, qui aggressorem; et ibi not. ar. ff. ad l.Aquil. Quemadmodum § Idem Labeo; et de incen. rui. et nau. l.3 § Quod ait; ar. ff. de bon. lib., Qui cum maior § Si libertus. Ignoscendum enim est illi qui qualitercunque sanguinem suum redimere voluit, ff. de bo. eo. qui mor. sibi consci. l.1 in fi. Nec solum cum infidelibus et dolosis possumus inimicos impugnare, sed per dolum, 22 q.2 Utilem; et 23 q.2 Dominus; ff. de capti. et postli. re. l.Nihil interest; nam et canes in ecclesia propter pacem ecclesie toleramus, 22 q.4 Quidam; exemplo Domini qui cum malis quandoque facit vindictam, 22 q.5 § Hinc notandum. Nam sicut videmus econtra, quod in bello iusto fideles obediunt, et iuvant infideles, 11 q.3 Iulianus; 23 q.1 § Ordo; et ad defensionem fructuum utimur arte mathematica, C. de Mathema. l.Eorum; cum tamen sit utroque testamento prohibita; et Paulus, ut ad sui defensionem provocaret Phariseos, dixit se Phariseum, Actuum 23 c. et petiit a preside milites quorum auxilio servaretur illesus, 23 q.4 § Sex in fi; et c. Maximianus; et Macha. qui fuerunt viri sancti et pugiles fidei inierunt pactum cum Romanis ut mutuo se iuvarent, ut 1 Mach 8 c.; et tamen Romani erant pagani; et Abraam confederavit se cum Eschol et eum secum duxit ad bellum et tamen non erat de lege sua, Gen. 14 et Mach.5 c.; et tempore necessitatis communicamus excommunicatis; et Salomon ligna pro edificando templo recepit ab infidelibus.

In contrarium videtur illud Paral. 19: 'Impio prebes auxilium, et his qui Dominum oderunt amicitia iungeris.' Et Rex Hierusalem fuit per Prophetam reprehensus quia voluit se iuvare cum regibus Israel, 37 et 23 q.3 c.1; et c. Sex; et c. Maximianus.

Sed ad primum respondetur, quod ibi bellum fuit iniustum. Et ad secundum, quod illi de Israel volebant inducere eos de Iudea et Hierusalem ad adorandum vitulos aureos, 23 q.3 Sex; et c. seq.; et 23 dist. c.1. Inter malos procuranda est divisio et dissensio. Nam (ut dicit beatus Gregorius in Moralibus) sicut noxium est si unitas desit bonis, sic est perniciosum si non desit malis. Perversos quippe unitas corroborat dum concordat, et tanto magis incorrigibiles quanto unanimes facit. Et ideo Paulus se Phariseum dixit, et divisio facta est inter Phariseos et Sadduceos, et liberationem consecutus est, Actuum 23; atque ibi dicit glosa quod sicut unitas bonorum utilis est sic malorum unitas semper bonis nociva est. Et propter tales Salvator Luc. 12 dicit quod non venit pacem dare in terras, sed separationem, unde Esaie [58]: 'Dissolve colligationes impietatis et fasciculos deprimentes.' Atque etiam inter hostes discordias procurare sapientis est ducis, ut vult dicere Vegetius de re milit. in c.10; et de hoc Isidorus in lib. 3. de sum. bo. c. 31, De malorum concordia.

CONSILIUM LXXII

An contra Sarracenos Hispanie sit bellum licitum. Et videtur quod eis volentibus in pace et quiete vivere non sit molestia inferenda, C. de pag. l.Christianis; pro hoc quod notat Innocentius, extra de voto, Quod super his; quia non est quis compellendus ad fidem, extra de Iud. c. Sicut; 23 q.1 Fidem; 45 di. De Iud. et c. Qui sincera; 23 q.4, c. pe. Et sic contra persequentes tantum videtur posse indici bellum, arg. 23 q. fi. Dispar; et pro hoc quod dicit apostolus ad Romanos: 'Vobis iam ultra bella non esse carnalia peragenda', 23 q.1 Nisi, in fi.; et ibi not. Archid. Et Malachie 1: 'Ab ortu,' inquit, 'solis usque ad occasum magnum est nomen meum in gentibus, et in omni loco sanctificatus, et offertur nomini meo oblatio munda.' Et de hoc in Chronica Ptolomei in Prologo. Et illud: 'Constitues eos principes super omnem terram, nec eorum potestas fuit arctata vel limitata, sed dilatata et ampliata; et excessit ab ortu usque ad occasum, et a mari usque ad mare, et a flumine usque ad finem orbis terrarum.' Et illud: 'Filium, quem constituit heredem universorum.' De hoc etiam [Odo] in sermone natalis Domini, 15 fo. Et ibi reges peccant in recipiendo ab eis tributum et dando eis pacem, et in fo. 20 quod forte per sexcentos annos oriens et occidens servierunt Christo usque ad tempus Machometi.

Sed quod contra Sarracenos illos bellum sit licitum, probatur sic: quia aut ipsi impugnant Christianos, et tunc non est dubium, ut in c. Dispar; nam tunc licitum est vim vi repellere, nam quod quis ad defensionem sui facit, iuste fecisse estimatur, de iusti. et iu. l.Ut vim; et ad l.Aquil. l.Scientiam § Qui cum aliter; extra de sen. excomm. c. Si vero; aut ipsi non impugnant, et adhuc dico quod bellum debet eis inferri quia verisimile est quod quandocunque ipsi oportunitatem habebunt, oppugnabunt et persequentur Christianos et ecclesiam, nam hec videntur eis naturaliter inesse. Unde dicit Magister in Scholastica Historia 1 c. De fuga [Agar]; quod illud quod scribitur Gen. 16 de patre eorum Ismael a quo ipsi descendunt, no. extra de Iude. et Sarra. c. Et si Iudeos; scilicet, manus eius contra omnes et manus eorum contra eum, et e regione fratrum suorum figet tentoria, verificatur in Sarracenis qui de genere suo descendunt, nam ipsi pugnant contra omnes et omnes pugnant contra eos. Et ideo licet modo sint in pace, quia forte non vident se posse nocere, quia tamen verisimile videtur quod in futurum pacem perturbabunt, non est eis indulgendum, 23 q.1 Noli, in fi. Et presupposito quod nunc et in futurum vellent omnem pacem, adhuc dico quod bellum est iustum et licitum. Nam tota illa provincia Hispanie fuit Christianorum et fuerunt ibi Ecclesie, monasteria et alia pia loca ubi laudabatur et colebatur Christus, et suberant sancte catholice ecclesie, et isti Saraceni violenter occupaverunt ea, nos spoliando permissione divina propter peccata nostra, 56. distinct. Si gens Anglorum, que licet pro maiori parte sit recuperata, ut not. 63 dist. Adrianus; adhuc tamen tenent partem, et sic cum nos agamus ad recuperationem patrie, qua sumus per violentiam spoliati, licitum est bellum, ut in c. Dispar. Et hoc debet iudicari defensio et non invasio. ar. C. unde vi. l.1; quia quod quis ob defensionem suam facit iuste fecisse estimatur, ut in lege preallegata Scientiam; et hoc etiam tenuit Innocentius in c. Quod super his; quod ubi terra fuerit aliquo tempore Christianorum bellum sit licitum. Ipse tamen magis stricte locutus est in materia ista, nam tenet quod iurisdictio et dominium etiam possit hodie esse penes infideles. Hostiensis tamen tenet contrarium. Et salva veritate videtur quod opinio Hostiensis sit verior, nam ratio Innocentii videtur habere locum in omni terra que hodie a Saracenis possidetur, non enim est locus ubi nomen Christi non fuerit laudatum et cultum. Unde de Apostolis legimus quod in omnem terram exivit sonus eorum, et in fines orbis terre verba eorum, 19 disti. Ita dominus. Et ipse Salvator dixit discipulis suis: 'Eritis mihi testes in omni Iudea et Samaria et usque ad ultimum terre,' 40 dist. Estimat; et pro hoc 21 distinct. In novo. De Christo enim verificatur quod omnes reges terre adorabunt eum et omnes gentes servient ei, 23 q.3, Displicet; et ideo dicit Hostiensis quod hodie non est iurisdictio, nec dominium, nec honor, nec potestas penes infideles, nam per adventum Christi translata sunt in Christianos. Transfertur enim regnum de gente in gentem propter iniustitias suas, 23 questio. fi. c. Si de rebus. Omnia enim subiecta sunt Christo, 'oves et boves et pecora campi', ut habetur in Psalmo 8, ubi dicit glosa quod omnia dixit quia nec celestia nec terrena dimisit, arg. 19 distinct. Si Romanorum. Per oves enim intelligimus Christianos, quorum in tempore Salvator dicit se esse pastorem, et fuit pastor bonus, quia animam suam posuit pro ovibus suis, Matthei 10 et 23, quest. 4, Tres [personas]. Item has commisit Petro et eius successoribus pascendas et monendas et ampliandas, 8 quest. 1, In scripturis. Sed per boves et pecora campi intelligimus Saracenos, qui tanquam bestie ratione carentes relicto Deo vero colunt idola, et vide in frumento in verbo Saracenis. Et Saraceni ad literam vocantur bestie quia et Ismael pater eorum vocatus est a Domino Onager, et fuit ratio, ut dicit Metodius, quia futurum erat quod qui de genere suo descenderent omnem bestiarum rabiem supergrederentur et mansuetarum numerus conteretur ab eis. In sacris enim locis (dicit ipse) iugulabunt sacerdotes, et ibidem cum mulieribus dormient, et ad sepulchra sanctorum iumenta alligabunt. Et hoc propter peccata Christianorum, ut hec narrat Magister in Historia Scholastica in predicta [c. de fuga] Agar.

Et vere omnem hanc sevitiam permittente Deo ipsi exercuerunt in illa provincia, argum. 6 quest. 1, Sciscitaris. Et licet iste bestie quo ad pastum Petro non videantur commisse, sunt tamen pedibus eius subiecte quo ad dominium et potestatem. Unde de ecclesia intelligitur illud quod Abraam dicit Sare uxori sue conquerenti de illa maledicta ancilla que eam contemnebat: 'Ecce', inquit, 'ancilla tua in manu tua, utere ea ut libet', Genes. 16. Per Saram enim ista sancta catholica ecclesia significatur. Per Agar ancillam illa maledicta secta Machometti, que ab ea traxit originem, 23 quest. 3, Quando; et c. Si ecclesia. Utatur ergo ista sancta ecclesia, que per Saram significatur, ista maledicta ancilla ut fuit usa illa beata Sara, eam affligendo, ut in predicto c. Si ecclesia. Utatur etiam, ut precepit dominus, eiiciendo et expellendo eam et filios eius ab hereditate et possessione ne partem habeant cum filiis liberis, 22 quest. 4, Recurrat; et c. Dixit Sara; et ca. Dicat. Nam cum sint filii ancille, et sic servi (partus enim sequitur ventrem, ff. de statu homin. l.In servorum); imo servi a Domino reprobati, ut extra de Iude. c. Si iudeos; non sunt capaces iurisdictionis, dominii, vel honoris, ff. de iudic. l.Cum pretor; et de arbit. l.Parvi § Sed si servum; et de acqui. re. do. liber homo. Et sic cum bellum istud tendat ad defensionem fidei, et recuperationem illius terre qua fuimus spoliati et in qua colebatur Christus, et sic ad ampliationem fidei, et eiectionem istius maledicte ancille et filiorum eius, nullus venit in dubium quin sit licitum. Et ideo ista sancta ecclesia et predicatores nostri semper approbaverunt istam guerram inducendo et hortando reges ad eam et concedendo illi multa subsidia spiritualia et temporalia, nec sine causa, quia concilium generale videtur equare merito facientes guerram istam, et Hierosolimitanam, 23 quest. fi. Pessimam. in fi.; et facit, quod not. Archid. 23 quest. 7, De rebus. Et quod decime concedantur pro actu tam pio facit, quia per hoc communis utilitas procuratur tam clericorum quam laicorum et ecclesiarum; ergo non est inconveniens ut contribuant in onere, arg. ff. ad l. Rho. de iactu. l.2 § Equissimum. Item quia pro redemptione captivorum etiam res sacre et sancte debent vendi, C. de sac. ecc. l.Sanciemus; 12 questio. 2, Sicut; et c. Aurum. Hoc autem agitur ut redimantur captivi et etiam ecclesie que per eos tenentur occupate, et ut alie defendantur in quibus melius est ante tempus occurrere quam post etc., C. quibus caus. in inte. resti. non est necess. l.fi.

Consilium LXXXVII

Queritur an princeps possit sine peccato expellere Iudeos et Saracenos de regno suo et eis bona auferre, et an papa hoc possit precipere principibus vel persuadere. Et primo videtur, quod non. Nam quiete Iudeis sub imperio degentibus molestia inferri non debet, nec eis bona auferri, C. de Iude. Nullus; et de paga. l.Christianus, et extra de Iude. [Sicut; et c.Iudei. Nam dominium et possessionem suarum habent c. de Iudeis, Nemo; in tantum, quod etiam collationes Christianas habere possunt extra de Iudeis], Multorum; et contra Christianos prescribunt, 16 questio. 3, Porro, et ibi not. Et si iust[e] possideant bona eis auferri non debent, ut not. 23 quest. 7, Si de rebus, et ibi Archidiaconus. Et princeps, si sine causa bona sua eis auferat, peccat, quia licet sit dominus quo ad protectionem non tamen eos sine iusta causa spoliat, ut not. C. de quadr. prescr. l.Bene a Zenone; et notat Innocentius, extra de immu. eccl., Quia plerique. Unde dicit ipse et Hostiensis, extra de voto, Quod super his, quod papa non debet eis bona auferre, imo quod debet eos tollerare, 45 dist. Qui sinceram, et extra de Iude. et Sara., Et si Iudeos. Et sit ratio, ut per eorum consortium eos Deo lucrari possimus, et 24 q.4, Infideles, et ar. 11 q.3, Ad mensam, et extra de divor. et c. Quanta. Maxime sunt tolerandi Iudei quia utiles sunt fidei nostre. Unde dicit Augustinus super Psalmo 40: 'Iudei tanquam capsarii nostri nobis serviunt. Nam studentibus nobis codices purgant, ut per hoc codices, in quibus sunt Lex et Prophete, per quos predicatus Christus est, et fidem nostram probemus cum paganis et aliis incredulis. Nam cum codices nostri eis sunt suspecti, melius eos per codices inimicorum convincimus.' Et Gregorius in Omelia Joannis dicit quod in fine mundi a Christo illuminabuntur. Et si de toto mundo expellerentur non remanerent aliqui, cum tamen lex dicat quod tunc reliquie Israel salve fient. Et quod tolerari debeant probat Augustinus super Psal. [40], ubi dicit quod fuit figuratum in illo Cain, qui fratrem suum occidit, et ideo accepit signum ne interficeretur, ut sic iste perversus populus sit signatus ne occidatur, imo toleretur.

Sed licet privata persona non debeat eis molestiam inferre videtur quod princeps possit maxime Iudeis, quia servi sunt facti per mortem Christi, extra de Iude, Et si Iudeos; quod fuit mandatum executioni per Constantium, ut notat Hostiensis eo. ti. c. Consuluit; et ex hoc dicit Archidiaconus 45 di. Qui sinceram, quod princeps qui est eorum dominus potest eos vendere, ergo multo magis expellere, ar. C. si servus asportandus veneat, l.1 et 2. Et ob istam etiam rationem dicit idem Archidiaconus 54 di.

Fraternitatem, quod potest eis auferre bona cum non habeant ea nisi ut peculium; allegat extra Iudeis. Iudei, ubi dicit, quod si convertantur non sint eis bona auferenda; ergo a contrario sensu, si non convertantur, sic. Melius facit eo. ti. c. Sicut, ubi dicit quod non sunt molestandi, nec privandi bonis sine licentia terrene potestatis; ergo cum licentia sic. Preterea isti sustinentur ex pietate et gratia, ut dicitur in c. Et si Iudeos. Non ergo debet trahi ad necessitatem, ff.de offi. procon. l.Solent in fi., nam sufficit si vel in paucis amici laboribus consulatur, C. de ne. ge. l.Tutori. Nec est de quo possint conqueri quia habuerunt gratiam velut alieni, ut dicit Boetius in lib. de consolatione. Et hoc videtur verum ubi Christianis imminet periculum vel scandalum, ut notat Innocentius, extra de voto, Quod super his, nam cum abusi fuerint gratia privilegium merentur amittere tanquam ingrati, ut in c. Et si Iudeos, et apparet de gravamine ecclesiarum, quia non solvunt decimas de possessionibus suis. Et ideo domini deberent compelli ad locanda predia talibus qui decimas solvant, extra de decimis, c. De terris et c. Quibusdam; de usur. c. Quanto. Et satis figuratum videtur in illa ancilla a qua ipsi descendunt, quia eo quod superbe et ingrate se habuit ad liberam per quam ecclesia designatur, fuit expulsa. Nam dictum fuit: 'Eiice ancillam et filium eius,' 23 q.3 Si ecclesia; licet ubi quiete viverent et non esset scandalum non videtur quod papa hoc deberet precipere vel suadere principibus, per ea que notantur in dictum capitulum Quod super his, et nihil ad eum de his qui foris sunt, extra de divor. Gaudemus. Tamen Gregorius in registro videtur comminari prelatis Sardinensibus si paganos rusticos habuerint, et precipit quod augeant eius pensiones ut per hoc redeant ad tramitem veritatis, et pars illius epistole est 23 questione septima, Iam vero. Sed in alia epistola quam mittit procuratori patrimonii aliter videtur loqui de Iudeis, quia non differt quod non habeant Iudeos, et quod non augmentet eis pensiones, sed quod promittat eis pensionis remissionem ut per hoc citius convertantur.

CONSILIUM XCI

Venit in dubium an Saraceni debeant compelli ad solutionem decimarum de terris ab eis possessis, et qualiter debeant compelli. Et pro Saracenis facit quia nunquam solverunt. Item, quia terre ille semper fuerunt Saracenorum. Pro hoc ultimo facit extra de usu., Quanto, ad finem sumpto ar. a contrario, etc.

Credo quod tenentur, nam cum decime sint tributum, 16 q.1, Decime, a quolibet possessore sunt solvende, extra de decimis, Pastoralis; C. sine censu, vel reliquiis. l.2 et 3; etiam infideli, extra de decimis, c. De terris et c. Tua. Cum ergo ipse universorum sit dominus, ut in Psalmo: 'Domini est terra et plenitudo eius,' [ut] dicto c. Tua, a quocunque terra excolatur decima ei solvenda est, ar. C. de anno. et tribu. l.1. lib. 10. Imo dominus terre est per censuram ecclesiasticam compellendus ut talibus terras suas det excolendas qui sine difficultate ecclesiis decimas solvant, ut eod. tit. In aliquibus, quod satis videtur de iure, maxime secundum Innocentium qui exemplificat in Saracenis. Non obstat consuetudo in decimis predialibus, ut c. In aliquibus, et plene notat Iohannes Andree in rubrica de decimis, lib. 6, nec obstat quod solvunt regi, nam si quod uni debetur alteri solvatur, non contingit liberatio, C. de solu.invito; extra de iureiu. c. Eam te. Et decime in laicum cadere non possunt, ut eo. c. Ad hoc, et l.Quamvis; imo rex recipiendo videtur sacrilegium committere, 16 q.7, Decimas, et extra de decimis, Tua. Non obstat quod dicitur quod terra ista semper fuit Saracenorum quia non est verum, imo totum quicquid est circa mare fuit Christianorum, et sic recuperatum debet redire ad pristinam naturam, ff. de relig. et sump. fune. c. Cum loca; 7 q.1, Pastoralis. Et posito quod non fuisset Christianorum, tamen ex quo ad dominium Christi est redacta, debet regi lege divina per quam sunt decime institute, ut in cap. Parochianos. Nec negari potest quod hodie est Christianorum, et Saraceni solum sint laboratores vel coloni. Nec obstat argumentum contrarium, quod posset sumi in c. Quanto, de usur., quia induceret contrarietatem iuris et peccatum contra ea que not. in l.Conventiculam, C. de episc. et cler.

Ad secundum, qualiter debeant compelli, dic uno modo ut in c. In aliquibus, scilicet ut compellantur domini non tradere eis terras ad laborandum; secundo modo secundum formam decretalis Postulasti, extra de Iude.

CONSILIUM CCLXIV

Illa videtur probabilior sententia quod princeps absque legitima causa pacificos Iudeos, Sarracenos, et alios paganos de terris suis non possit expellere.

Et primo, quia iuris naturalis est et divini quod quecunque vult princeps sibi iuste fieri et faciat aliis maxime suis servis aut tributariis, Matth. 7 c. di. 1. ca. Humanum; nec aliis faciat quod nollet sibi fieri, extra de maior. et obe. c. Dilecti. Sed ipse nollet de regno expelli; ergo non alios de regno expellat. Tenetur etiam diligere Iudeos et Sarracenos inquantum sue nature participes nedum in anima sed etiam in corpore, ut est expressum de peni. dist. 2 Charitas. in verb. non illi, et ver. seq. ibi quomodo nos in eorum peccatis et periculis cogitamus, et sic nobis subveniri optamus, et ita eis subvenimus., et infra: 'Quapropter, charissime, ita tota dilectione satage ut bonum quod tibi conferri vis, velis et proximo.' Expellere ergo tales absque ratione contra precepta charitatis aperte est. Dilectio enim proximi malum expulsionis, vel aliud non operatur, ad Rom. 13, 'et charitas non agit perperam,' 1 ad Corin.13, 'et recta voluntas iniquum non agit,' in prealleg. c. Charitas. Et tale ius divinum et naturale indispensabile est quia impermutabile, instit. de iure naturali, § Sed naturalia; dist. 6, His ita; etiam per Papam, quia eius permutatio necessario peccatum implicat; facit quod no. de iureiuran., Et si Christus, in glosa Quedam; et naturam bonam immutat, quod est impossibile, dist. 13. § 1, di. 1, Ius naturale. Hinc est etiam quod ex isto iure et charitate in necessitate eis subvenire et eleemosynam facere tenemur, 42 dist. Quiescamus; 16 q. 1, Si cupis; 86 di. Non satis.

Secundo, hosti capto debetur misericordia, presertim ubi pacis perturbatio non timetur, multo fortius talis misericordia facienda est servo tributario ne expellatur, 23 q.1, c. Noli. Principes enim iubentur timentibus et obsequentibus impendere dilectionem, nihil facere cupiditate nocendi, sed omnia charitate consulendi, nihil in[m]aniter, nihil inhumaniter, 23 q.5, Prodest. Et quod agendum est non ex furore sed ex charitate agendum est, 12 q.2, Fraternitas.

Tertio, eadem ratione qua non debemus Iudeos et paganos et Sarracenos pacificos rebus suis spoliare, eadem ratione nec eorum habitaculis et [terra] nativa privare. Hec probantur per nota. 23 q.7, c. Si de rebus, in glosa Per hoc. Et quod possident, iure gentium possident, sive res, sive loca, sive iurisdictione, et sic iuste et iusticia fori non poli, 14 quest. 4, Quod dicam; extra de verbor. significa., Ius dictum est, sicut hoc clare tenet Innocentius, extra de voto, et voti redempt., Quod his; et facit 23 quest. 5, Si propterea, ibi vindicavit iustissime. Et quod non possint nisi persecutores fuerint expelli facit bene a sensu contrario, 23 quest. 7, Si qui; alias est sub capitulo Si de rebus. Et innocenti[e], maxime regum, est nemini malum inferre, 23 quest. 5, ca. Non est; 6 quest. 1, Sapiens. Omni Christiane inest religioni lenitas et mansuetudo, et crudelitas ei contraria est signanter, 23 quest. 5, Unum solum.

Item tertio, [mater] istorum Agarenorum Agar et filius eius Ismael pater Agarenorum ideo expulsi sunt a Sara, Genes. 16, quod et ipsa persequebatur dominam suam, et ipse fratrem suum Isaac, de qua utraque persequutione clare loquitur Augustinus, 24. quest. 4, Si ecclesia, et [32] questio. 4, Recurrat, ubi superbus Ismael erexit cervicem, et voluit seducere fratrem suum ludens, quia cogebat Isaac adorare luteas imagines, quas faciebat, ut dicit glosa que incipit Ismael. Ergo ubi Agareni humiliter conversantur, et non decipiunt simplices Christianos colere suum luteum Machometum, non propterea expellendi sunt sed recipiendi, sicut dicit angelus Agar, 23 questio 4, Quando bene facit.

Item quarto, pagani et Iudei inter oves Christi computantur creatione, gubernatione, et redemptione ex parte Christi. Unde Dominus in Evange. Ioan. 10. capit.: 'Alias oves habeo que non sunt ex hoc ovili,' scilicet ecclesie. Unde et Papa super eos potestatem habet sicut super oves suas, quas ei inter alia commisit Christus, Ioan.ultim.: 'Pasce oves meas,' non distinguens inter has et illas, extra de maio. et obe., Solite § penult.; et sic tenet Innocentius, per cap. Quod super his, eo. tit. Cum ergo papa eos pascere debeat et verbo et exemplo et humanitate non rebelles, non ergo debet eos impugnare, nec permittere ut ledantur, extra de natis ex libero ventre. capit. una. ubi de hoc.

Quinto, infideles non terroribus, non asp[e]ritatibus, non violentiis sunt trahendi ad fidem neque expulsionibus, sed blanditiis et muneribus, ut integra sit forma iustitie et libertas arbitrii, 45 dist., Qui sincera, quod bene facit, et ead. dist. c. De iude; et 23 quest. 4, c. ulti., quod optime facit, ubi etiam infidelis vocatur proximus. Debet autem homo diligere proximum sicut seipsum, ut quam poterit hominem beneficentie consolatione, vel informatione doctrine, vel discipline coerctione adducat ad colendum Deum. Et si sic Iudei iuste ubilibet expellerentur, et deficeret in eis verbum Isaie et Pauli, nec adimpleretur quod eorum reliquie salve fient, ad Roma. 9 c. quod not. 28 quest. 1, Iudeorum, in glosa 1; et fidei nostre testimonium non preberent, sicut probat Eusebius, libr.3. Ecclesiastice Historie, cap.7, pulchre dicens: 'Propter hoc Iudaica gens pro culpa perfidie de regno suo pulsa est et dispersa per terras, ut eius fidei, cuius inimici sunt, ubique testes fieri cogerentur perdito quippe templo et sacrificio, ipso quoque regno, in paucis veteribus sacramentis nomen genusque custodirent, ut permixti gentibus sine discretione dispereant, et testimonium veritatis admittant, velut Cain profugus a facie Domini.' Et Augustinus in sermonibus Epiphanie: 'Ideo Iudeos non occidit, id est, de terris non penitus perdidit, ne obliviscantur legis quam propterea legendo reminiscuntur, ut sibi sumant iudicium, et nobis prebeant testimonium veritatis.'

Sexto, facit verbum Apostoli docentis dominos qualiter de servis suis obedientibus se habere debeant, ad Ephes. ult. c. ibi 'et vos domini eadem facite illis,' scilicet servis, 'remittentes minas scientes, quia et illorum et noster dominus est in celis, et personarum acceptio non est apud Deum,' et ad Colos. ult. in principio: 'Domini, quod iustum est et equum servis prestate scientes quod et vos dominum habetis in celis.' Unde sicut infideles Sarraceni vel alii inter nos habitantes a nobis sunt pro suis sceleribus puniendi, extra de rap. in archiepiscopatu, sic sine causa [non] sunt expellendi vel puniendi, 56 distinct., Satis perversum; extra de constit. c.2. Item sicut non sunt infideles de suis possessionibus expellendi, ita nec eis sunt auferende, sicut etiam nec sunt de suis antiquis habitationibus expellendi, 26 distin. Deinde, extra de Iudeis. Iudei. 2 § 1 ibi a possessionibus suis, et c. Sicut Iudei, et c. Et si Iudeos, in princ. ibi pietas Christiana receptet et sustineat cohabit[at]ionem illorum, ergo non expellantur. Item filii Israel non eiecerunt Iebuseos de Ierusalem, Iudi. 1. 11 questi. 3, Nolite ergo, etc.

Septimo, casus videntur expressi C. de sacrific. paga. l.Christianos, ubi dicitur quod talibus quiete degentibus nullam debemus facere molestiam, et 23 quest. 8, Dispar, ibi 'qui Christianos persequuntur'. Ergo a contrario sensu, si non persequuntur non sit molestia neque guerra, sic arguit glosa ibi et facit 16 questio. 3, Porro, ibi 'ceterum ut paganorum et incredulorum furor in causa est,' etc. Ergo a contrario sensu, etc. et quod ibi notatur. Preterea ibi scriptum est: 'Celum celi Domino, terram autem dedit filiis hominum,' ubilibet autem habitare licitum est cuicunque, etiam servo dummodo tributum solvat debitum domino ratione dominii, extra de censi. Omnis, 11 questi. 1, Magnum. Ergo nulli negandum est quod ius humane societatis concedit. arg. bon. 13 questi. 1, c. Notandum; facit 5 dist. Ad eius vero. Item causa expulsionis Ammorreorum Cananeorum et Iebuseorum ab eorum terris per filios Israel peccata eorum fuerunt, maxime idololatria que est contra legem nature, que clamat unum Deum, ad Roman. 1 ibi 'invisibilia Dei,' etc. Sed Iudei et Sarraceni non sunt idololatre, sed alias infideles, neque tales publici hostes principum regentium Christianorum;

ergo non debent expelli, argum. expressum 23 quest. 5 § Hinc notandum; et Iosue 5 et 7; et Deuteron. 7; Genes. 15. Hec sufficiant canoniste et theologo grosso; gentibus vero vos subtilia argumenta legalia et canonica adiungetis.

Consilium CCCXXXIII

Qualiter puniatur Iudeus cognoscens carnaliter Christianam? Fateri quidem oportet prohibitum esse Iudeum Christiane coniungi, quia cum matrimonium sit communicatio divini iuris, ff.de ritu nupt. l.1; de crim. expi. he. adversus; hoc casu, cum non sit, constat matrimonium non esse, 27 questi. 1, Cave; et talis contrahens tanquam adulter puniretur, C. de Iude. Ne quis Christianam. Sed de alia commixtione Iudei cum Christiana, licet sit prohibita extra, non occurrit ius expressum dicens eum tanquam adulterum puniri. Etsi forte diceretur arguendo quod si puniretur talis commixtio sub velamine matrimonii commissa, ut supra dictum est, fortius sine velamine tali, ut ff. de adulter., Si adulterium cum incestu. Sed hec multum non cogit. Primo, quia commixtionem illicitam committit et matrimonii sacramento iniuriam facit, C. ne sanctum Bap. rei l.1, secus si solum coitus concupiscentiam facit, in Authent. de restit. et ea que parit. § unum, Si quidem, et qui mo. na. effi. sui in princip.; et hoc intelligo cessantibus aliis circumstantiis que ad hanc commixtionem alterius peccati deteriorationem adiiciunt, ut de raptu, stupro, et incestu, tunc enim oportet ex alterius criminis adiectione gravius puniri, l.1. de rap. vir. Hec autem cessant in accessu ad mulierem, de iniuri. l.Item apud Labeonem § Si quis virgines; ideo non est talis ut adulter puniendus capitaliter, C. de adul. que adulterium, ubi not.

Non dico tamen, quod hec feda commixtio civiliter ad arbitrium iudicantis non sit aliqualiter punienda, ff. de effracto. l.1 § Expilatores, et quod confessus est tortus et non questioni positus non videtur ei obesse, quia de vulgaribus tantum confessus est, et quia nullis i[u]diciis precedentibus confessus fuit, et contra privilegium concessum Hebreis per reginam M. unde quod dixit religionem iudicantis non instruxit, ff. de questio. divus. ubi no. Advertat tamen dominus iudex, quia non severitate gloria affectanda, sed in levioribus promptus ad levitatem iudex esse debet, et in gravioribus severitatem legis debet cum aliquo temperamento benigne prosequi.

Ego Oldradus predicta scripsi et sigillum apposui. Sed Dominus R. de Apulea, et Dominus Ant. de Cruce, qui tunc preerant in officio iudicatus Avinion., dictum Iudeum in amissione virilium condemnaverunt, cuius nomen erat Pandonus, et ego vidi virilia incisa ante palatium.

APPENDIX
BIBLIOGRAPHY
INDEX

Appendix

The following is a preliminary check-list of manuscripts and printed editions of Oldradus' *Consilia*, either complete collections or individual items, which those interested in the subject of consilia in general or Oldradus in particular may find useful. For notices of many of the MSS, apart from catalogues of individual libraries, see *Verzeichnis der Handschriften zum römischen Recht*, 4 vols., ed. Gero Dolezalek (Frankfurt, 1972). Some of the printed editions listed below, and their locations, are taken from Guido Kisch, *Consilia*, pp. 69–70. For incunabula to be found in Italian libraries, see Ministero della Pubblica Istruzione, *Indici e cataloghi*, nuova serie, 1, *Indice generale degli incunaboli delle biblioteche d'Italia*, compiled by E. Valenziani and E.Cerulli, 4 [M-R] (Rome, 1965), p. 157, nos. 6986–6989. Some early locations of incunabula are noted in L. Polain, *Catalogue général des incunables des bibliothèques publiques de France* (Nendeln, Liechtenstein: Kraus-Thomson, 1970) 15:8560–8563b, and in Henri Baudrier, *Bibliographie Lyonnaise* (Lyons and Paris, 1901–1906) 5:419, 454; 6:162.

Manuscripts

Basel, Öffentliche Bibliothek der Universität Basel, C.III.14.

Bordeaux, Bibliothèque de la Ville, 404, ff. 4v-168v.

Bologna, Biblioteca Albornoziana del' Collegio di Spagna, 83.

Bologna, Biblioteca Albornoziana del' Collegio di Spagna, 207.

Cordoba, Cathedral, 40, 14th c., with many quaestiones of Oldradus (Antonio Garcia y Garcia, *Catalogo de los manuscritos e incunables de la catedral de Cordoba*, Salamanca, 1972).

Cordoba, Cathedral, 108 (a few folios of Oldradus).

Dresden, Sächsischelandesbibliothek, B87, ff. 209–235v.

Florence, Biblioteca Nazionale Centrale, fondo Magliabecchi, XXIX, 174.

Graz, Universitätsbibliothek, ff. 290–332.

Kansas, Kenneth Spencer Research Library, University of Kansas Libraries, G18. Late 14th-early 15th c. (261 consilia).

Kues (Cues) 277 (273 consilia); J. Marx, *Verzeichnis der Handschriften-Sammlung des Hospitals zu Cues*, p. 268.

Lucca, Biblioteca Capitolare Feliniana, curia arcivescovile, 301.

Lucca, Biblioteca Capitolare Feliniana, curia arcivescovile, 398.

Lucca, Biblioteca Capitolare Feliniana, curia arcivescovile, 415.

Oxford, New College, 217, ff. 171–351. 15th c. (262 consilia).

Paris, BN, Lat. 4276A.

Paris, BN, Lat. 14335 (244 consilia); see *Le catalogue de la bibliothèque de l'abbaye de Saint Victor de Paris de Claude de Grandrue 1514* (Editions du Centre national de la recherche scientifique, Paris, 1983), p. 70: 'Allegationes domini Oldrandi de Laude super diversis dubiis orientibus quarum sunt tituli ducenti quadraginta quatuor.'

Rome, Biblioteca Angelica, 275, a miscellany with a consilium of Oldradus, ff. 167–170.

Stockholm, Kathedralbibliothek, F. mai. 2, 15th c. (c.1460).

Tübingen, Universitätsbibliothek, 17, 15th c.

Turin, Biblioteca Nazionale, H.I.9.

Uppsala, Universitetsbiblioteket, C.537, ff. 225r–334v.

Uppsala, Universitetsbiblioteket, C.545, ff. 1–198v.

Vatican City, Bib. Vat., Vat. lat. 2653. Written in 1426 by John Vlessentop in Rome (273 consilia).

Vatican City, Bib. Vat., Ross. 1096. Early 15th c. (274 consilia).

Vatican City, Bib. Vat., Urb. lat. 1132, f. 141; a miscellany with a consilium of Oldradus, f. 141.

Vatican City, Bib. Vat., Vat.lat. 8068; a miscellany with two consilia of Oldradus, ff. 107r and 188v.

Vatican City, Bib. Vat., Vat.lat. 2642; a miscellany with a consilium of Oldradus, f. 133.

Zeitz, Stiftsbibliothek, no shelf mark, ff. 2–157v (dated 1409).

Printed Editions

Rome. 1472. Adam Rot of the diocese of Metz. 227ff. (264 consilia). Hain 9932. (Locations: Huntington Library, San Marino, California; Stadsbibliotheek van Maastricht; British Library, London; Bibliothèque Nationale, Paris; Biblioteca Nazionale Centrale, Florence; Biblioteca Nazionale Vittorio Emanuele II, Naples; Biblioteca Comunale, Perugia; Biblioteca Comunale "Joppi," Udine.)

S. Marcum. 1476. Hain 9933 ['Est sine dubio ed. subsequus'].

Rome [Vitus Puecher]. St. Mark. 1478. (dedicated to Johannes Franciscus de Pavinis, prof.theol., auditor causarum sacr. pal., by Alfonsus de Sotto). 229ff. (333 consilia). Hain 9934. (Locations: Biblioteca del Seminario Vescovile, Bressanone; Biblioteca Capitolare Feliniana, Lucca; Biblioteca Casanatense, Rome; Biblioteca Nazionale, Rome; Biblioteca Capitolare, Trent; Jewish Theological Seminary of America, New York; Library of Congress, Washington).

[Basle] 19 Nov. 1481. Eberhard Frommolt. (264 consilia). Hain 9935. (Locations: British Library, London; Harvard College Library, Cambridge, Mass; Cambridge University Library, Cambridge, Eng.; Universitätsbibliothek, Basel; Universitätsbibliothek, Freiburg im Breisgau).

Venice. 18 June 1490. (dedicated to J.F. de Pavinis; cf. Hain 9934). Bernardinus de Tridino de Monteferrato. 128ff. Hain 9936. (Locations: British Library, London; University of Iowa, Iowa City, Iowa; Staats- und Stadtbibliothek, Augsburg; Biblioteca Nacional, Mexico City; Biblioteca Capitolare e del Seminario Lolliniana Gregoriana, Belluno; Biblioteca della Badia della SS. Trinità, Cava; Biblioteca dell' Accademia Concordiana, Rovigo; Biblioteca Capitolare, Verona; Biblioteca Comunale Bertoliana, Vicenza; Universitätsbibliothek, Basel).

Ugo de Rugeriis. Bologna. 1495. Hain 9937.

Venice. 19 April 1499 (dedicated to J.F. de Pavinis; cf. Hain 9934). Bernardinus Stagnin de Tridino de Monteferrato. Hain 9938. (Locations: Oxford, All Soul's College; Law School Library, Harvard University; Biblioteca Capitolare, Padua).

Lyons n.d. (Locations: Universitätsbibliothek, Basel, M e II 4 Nr.3).

Venice, December 1503 (dedicated to J.F. de Pavinis) "in domo Andree de Turresnis de Asula" (Locations: Trinity Hall, Cambridge University).

Pavia 1503 (Locations: Universitätsbibliothek, Basel; Universitätsbibliothek, Freiburg im Breisgau).

Milan 1515 (Locations: Universitätsbibliothek, Freiburg im Breisgau).

Venice 1515 (see Karl Schulz, *Katalog der Bibliothek des Reichsgerichts*, II [Leipzig, 1890]).

Lyons, 5 May 1520, Vincent de Portonariis.

Lyons, 1535. Vincent Portunaris and J. Giunta. (Locations: Law School Library, Harvard University).

Venice, 1543. (333 consilia). (Locations: Spencer Research Library, University of Kansas, Lawrence, Kansas; St. John's Seminary Library, Brighton, Mass.).

Lyons, 1550. (333 consilia) (dedicated to J.F. Panvinis). (Locations: Universitätsbibliothek, Basel; Trinity College, Cambridge University; University of California, Berkeley, California).

Venice, "apud Franciscum Zilettum," 1570. (Locations: Law School Library, Harvard University).

Venice, "apud Franciscum Zilettum," 1571. Dedicated to cardinal Bobba by Rainaldus Corsus. (333 consilia). (Locations: Institute for Advanced Study, Princeton; Law School Library, Harvard University; Library of Congress, Washington; University of California, Los Angeles, California).

Frankfurt, "per Petrum Fabricium, impensis Sigismundi Feyrabent," 1576. (Locations: Law School Library, Harvard University; Trinity Hall, Cambridge University; Bibliothèque Nationale, Paris).

Venice, "ex officina Damiani Zenari," 1585 (Locations: Law School Library, Harvard University; Biblioteca Vaticana, Rome; Biblioteca Casanatense, Rome; Law Library, University of Minnesota).

Bibliography

Ahmad, Aziz. *A History of Islamic Sicily*. Edinburgh: Edinburgh University Press, 1975.

Alexander, Paul J. "Byzantium and the Migration of Literary Works and Motifs: The Legend of the Last Roman Emperor." *Medievalia et Humanistica*, new series, 2 (1971) 47–68.

Amari, Michele. *Storia dei musulmani di Sicilia*. 3 vols. in 5. Catania: R. Prampolini, 1933–1939.

Ames, Ruth M. "The Source and Significance of 'The Jew and the Pagan.'" *Medieval Studies* 19 (1957) 37–47.

Anfosso, Luigi. "Oldrado da Ponte e le sue opere." *Archivio storico per la città e communi del circondario di Lodi* 32 (1913) 101–116.

Ascheri, Mario. "Analecta manoscritta consiliare (1285–1354)." *Bulletin of Medieval Canon Law*, new series, 15 (1985) 61–94.

—. *I consilia dei giuristi medievali*. Siena: Edizione "Il Leccio," 1982.

Augustine (St.). *Sancti Aurelii Augustini enarrationes in Psalmos*, ed. Eligius Dekkers and Iohannes Fraipont. Corpus christianorum, series latina, 38. Turnhout: Brepols, 1956.

Baluze, Etienne. *Vitae paparum Avenionensium*, ed. Guillaume Mollat. 4 vols. Paris: Letouzey et Ané, 1914–1927.

Bardinet, L. "Condition civile des Juifs du Comtat Venaissin pendant le séjour des papes à Avignon 1309–1378." *Revue historique* 12 (1880) 1–47.

—. "Les Juifs du Comtat Venaissin au moyen-âge. Leur rôle économique et intellectuel." *Revue historique* 14 (1880) 1–60.

Baron, Salo Wittmayer. "Plenitude of Apostolic Powers and Medieval Jewish Serfdom." In *Ancient and Medieval Jewish History: Essays*, ed. Leon A. Feldman, pp. 286–307. New Brunswick: Rutgers University Press, 1972.

Baronius, Caesar. *Annales ecclesiastici*. 37 vols. Bar-le-Duc: Guérin, 1864–1888.

Bauer, J. "Les conversions juives dans le Comtat-Venaissin." *Revue des études juives* 50 (1905) 91–111.

Baumgärtner, Ingrid. "Consilia – Quellen zur Familie in Krise und Kontinuität." In *Die Familie als sozialer und historischer Verband*, ed. Peter-Johannes Schuler, pp. 43–66. Sigmaringen: Jan Thorbecke, 1987.

—. *Martinus Garatus Laudensis, Ein italienischer Rechtsgelehrter des 15. Jahrhunderts*. Dissertationen zur Rechtsgeschichte 2. Cologne/Vienna: Bohlau, 1986.

Bede. *Venerabilis Baedae opera historica*, ed. Charles Plummer. Oxford: Clarendon Press, 1896.

—. *Bedae venerabilis opera*, pars II, *Opera exegetica*, 1: *Libri quator in principium Genesis usque ad nativitatem Isaac et eiectionem Ismahelis adnotationum*, ed. Charles W. Jones. Corpus christianorum, series latina, 118A. Turnhout: Brepols, 1967.

Bibliorum sacrorum cum glossa ordinaria ... et postilla Nicolae Lyrani ... tomus sextus. Paris, 1590.

Blumenkranz, Bernhard. *Les auteurs chrétiens latins du moyen-âge sur les juifs et le judaisme*. Paris: Mouton, 1963.

—, ed. *Histoire des Juifs en France*. Paris: Privat, 1977.

—. *Juifs et chrétiens dans le monde occidentale, 430–1096*. Paris: Mouton, 1960.

Bofarull, Francisco de. "Jaime I el conquistador y la comunidad judía de Montpeller." *Boletín de la Real Academia de Buenas Letras de Barcelona* 5 (1909–1910) 484–492.

Boswell, John. *The Royal Treasure: Muslim Communities Under the Crown of Aragon in the Fourteenth Century*. New Haven: Yale University Press, 1977.

Bramon, Dolors. *Contra Moros i Jueus: Formació i estratègia d'unes discriminacions al país Valencià*. Valencia: E. Climent, 1981.

Bresc, Henri. *Livre et société en Sicile (1299–1499)*. Palermo: [Luxograph], 1971.

Burns, R.I. *Muslims, Christians and Jews in the Crusader Kingdom of Valencia*. Cambridge: Cambridge University Press, 1984.

Bussi, Emilio. "La condizione giuridica dei musulmani nel diritto canonico." *Rivista di storia del diritto italiano* 8 (1935) 459–494.

Butzer, Karl W., Elizabeth K. Butzer, Juan F. Mateu. "Medieval Muslim Communities of the Sierra de Espadan, Kingdom of Valencia." *Viator* 17 (1986) 339–420.

Chejne, Anwar G. *Islam and the West: The Moriscos, A Cultural and Social History*. Albany: State University of New York Press, 1983.

Cipriani, Renata, ed. *Codici miniati dell'Ambrosiana: Contributo a un catalogo*. Vicenza: N. Pozza, 1968.

Codicis sacratissimis imper. Iustiniani pp. Augusti lib. XII Accursii commentariis ... illustrati. Geneva: 1625.

Cohen, Gerson D. "Esau as Symbol in Early Medieval Thought." In *Jewish Medieval and Renaissance Studies*, ed. Alexander Altmann, pp. 19–48. Philip W. Lown Institute of Advanced Judaic Studies, Brandeis University; Studies and Texts 4. Cambridge, Mass.: Harvard University Press, 1967.

Cole, Penny Jane. *The Preaching of the Crusades to the Holy Land, 1095–1270*. Doctoral diss., University of Toronto, 1985.

Coulon, Auguste and S. Clémencet. *Lettres secrètes et curiales du pape Jean XXII (1316–1334) relatives à la France*. Paris: E. de Boccard, 1913–1972.

Cutler, A.H. and H.E. Cutler. *The Jew as Ally of the Muslims*. South Bend, Indiana: University of Notre Dame Press, 1986.

Czerwinski, F.R. *The Teachings of the Twelfth and Thirteenth Century Canonists about the Jews*. Doctoral diss., Cornell University, 1972.

d'Alverney, Marie-Thérèse. "La connaissance de l'Islam au temps de Saint Louis." In *Septième centenaire de la mort de Saint Louis: Actes des colloques de Royaumont et de Paris (21–27 mai 1970)*, pp. 235–246. Paris: Société d'édition les Belles Lettres, 1976.

—. "La connaissance de l'Islam en Occident du IXe au milieu du XIIIe siècle." *L'Occidente e l'Islam nell' alto medioevo*. Settimane di studio del' Centro italiano di studi sull' alto medioevo 12, pp. 577–602. Spoleto: [s.n.], 1965.

Daniel, Norman. *The Arabs in Mediaeval Europe*. London: Longman, 1975; 2nd ed. 1979.

—. *Islam and the West: The Making of an Image*. Edinburgh: Edinburgh University Press, 1960.

Decretales D. Gregorii papae IX suae integritati una cum glossis restitutae. Lyons: 1584.

Decretum Divi Gratiani totius prope modum iuris canonici compendium summorumque pontificum decreta ... . Lyons: 1560.

Digestum Vetus D. Iustiniani sacratissimi principis ... cui praeter notissimos Accursii Florentini commentarios ... novae ... annotationes accesserunt, [Infortiatum ... , Digestum Novum ...]. 3 vols. Lyons: 1549–1550.

Dolezalek, Gero. "Quaestiones motae in Rota: Richterliche Beratungsnotizien aus dem vierzehnten Jahrhundert." *Proceedings of the Fifth International Congress of Medieval Canon Law, Salamanca, 21–25*

September 1976, ed. Stephan Kuttner and Kenneth Pennington. Città del Vaticano: Biblioteca Apostolica, 1980.

Dupuy, Pierre. *Histoire du differend d'entre le pape Boniface* VIII. *et Philippes le bel roy de France*. Paris: Cramoisy, 1655; rpt. Tuscon: Audax Press, 1963.

[Fastolf, Thomas]. *Dominorum de Rota decisiones novae, antiquae et antiquiores*. Lyons: 1562.

Fattal, Antoine. *Le statut légal des non-musulmans en pays d'Islam*. Beirut: Imprimerie catholique, 1958.

Fayen, Arnold. *Lettres de Jean* XXII *(1316-1334); textes et analyses*. Analecta vaticano-belgica, vols. 2 and 3. Rome: M. Bretschneider; Paris: H. Champion, 1908.

Fierens, Alphonse. *Lettres de Benoît* XII *(1334-1342); textes et analyses*. Analecta vaticano-belgica 4. Rome: M. Bretschneider; Paris: H. Champion, 1910.

Finke, Heinrich. *Acta Aragonensia: Quellen zur deutschen, italienischen, französischen, spanischen, zur Kirchen- und Kulturgeschichte aus der diplomatischen Korrespondenz Jaymes* I. *(1291-1327)*. 3 vols. Berlin and Leipzig: W. Rothschild, 1908.

Fletcher, R.A. "Reconquest and Crusade in Spain c.1050-1150." *Transactions of the Royal Historical Society*, 5th series, 37 (1987) 31-47.

Friedberg, Emil Albert. *Corpus Iuris Canonici*. 2 vols. Leipzig: Tauchnitz, 1879-1891; rpt. Graz: Akademische Druck- und Verlaganstalt, 1959.

Gilles, Henri. "Législation et doctrine canoniques sur les Sarrasins." *Islam et chrétiens du Midi (*XIIe-XIVe *s.)*. Cahiers de Fanjeaux, 18; Toulouse: E. Privat, 1983, pp. 195-213.

Giordanengo, G. "Note sur un manuscrit juridique du Midi de la France, (*Vat.Lat.* 2642)." *Revue historique de droit français et étranger* 49 (1971) 95-107.

Girard, Joseph and P. Pansier. *La Cour temporelle d'Avignon aux XIVe et XVe siècles*. Paris and Avignon: 1909.

Grassi, Giuseppina Nicolosi. "Analisi di manoscritti vaticani per uno studio dei 'Consilia' di Giovanni e Gaspare Calderini." *Rivista di storia del diritto italiano* 50 (1977) 127-212.

Grayzel, Solomon. "The Avignon Popes and the Jews." *Historia judaica* 2 (1940) 1-12.

—. *The Church and the Jews in the XIIIth Century*. Philadelphia: Dropsie College for Hebrew and Cognate Learning, 1933; rpt. New York: Hermon Press, 1966.

—. "The Papal Bull *Sicut judeis*." In *Studies and Essays in Honor of Abraham A. Neuman*, pp. 243-280. Leiden: Brill for the Dropsie College, Philadelphia, 1962.

Gregory (St.). *S. Gregorii Magni registrum epistularum*, ed. Dag Norberg. Corpus christianorum, series latina, 140. Turnhout: Brepols, 1982.

—. *S. Gregorii Magni Moralia in Iob*, ed. Mark Adraen. Corpus christianorum, series latina, 143-143B. 3 vols. Turnhout: Brepols, 1979-1985.

Hayez, Michel and Anne-Marie Hayez. "Juifs d'Avignon au tribunal de la cour temporelle sous Urbain v." *Provence historique* 23 (1973) 165-173.

Herde, Peter. "Christians and Saracens at the Time of the Crusades: Some Comments of Contemporary Medieval Canonists." *Studia Gratiana* 12 (1967) 359-376.

—. *Audientia litterarum contradictarum*. Bibliothek des Deutschen Historischen Instituts in Rom 31-32. 2 vols. Tübingen: M. Niemeyer, 1970.

Horn, Norbert. "Die legistische Literatur der Kommentatoren und der Ausbreitung des gelehrten Rechts." In *Handbuch der Quellen und*

Literatur der neueren europäischen Privatrechtsgeschichte, 1: *Mittelalter (1100–1500): Die gelehrten Rechte und die Gesetzgebung*, ed. Helmut Coing, pp. 261–364 [Consilium: pp. 336–340]. Munich: Beck, 1973.

Indices canonum titulorum et capitulorum corporis iuris canonici, ed. Xaverio Ochoa and Aloisio Diez. Rome: Commentarium pro Religionis, 1964.

Indices corporis iuris civilis ..., ed. by Ugo Nicolini and Franca Sinatti d'Amico. Milan: Giuffrè, 1964–70.

Innocentii quarti pontificis maximi in quinque libros decretalium. Frankfurt: 1570.

Isidore. *Isidori Hispalensis episcopi Etymologiarum sive originum libri* XX, ed. W.M. Lindsay. 2 vols. Oxford: Clarendon Press, 1911.

Jacoby, David. "Venice, The Inquisition and the Jewish Communities of Crete in the early 14th Century." *Studi veneziani* [Florence] 12 (1970) 127–144; rpt. in David Jacoby, *Recherches sur la Méditerranée orientale du* XII*e au* XV*e siècle: peuples, sociétés, économies*. London: Variorum Reprints, 1979.

Josephus. *Josephus*, ed. H. St. J. Thackeray *et al*. Loeb Classical Library. 9 vols. London: W. Heinemann, 1926–1965.

Kedar, Benjamin Z. "Canon Law and the Burning of the Talmud." *Bulletin of Medieval Canon Law* 9 (1979) 79–82.

—. *Crusade and Mission: European Approaches toward the Muslims*. Princeton: Princeton University Press, 1984.

Kisch, Guido. *Consilia: Eine Bibliographie der juristischen Konsiliensammlungen*. Basle: Helbing and Lichtenhahn, 1970.

Kremer, Marita. *Manuscripta iuridica*. Die Handschriften der murhardschen Bibliothek der Stadt Kassel und Landesbibliothek 2, ed. Ludwig Denecke. Wiesbaden: Harrassowitz, 1969.

Kriegel, Maurice. "Prémarranisme et inquisition dans la Provence des XIIIe et XIVe siècles." *Provence historique* 27 (1977) 313-323.

Kuttner, Stephan. "Cardinalis: The History of a Canonical Concept," *Traditio* 3 (1945) 129-214.

Lang, Carl, ed. *Flavi Vegeti Renati epitoma rei militaris*. Leipzig: Teubner, 1885.

Liebeschutz, H. "The Crusading Movement and Its Bearing on the Christian Attitude Towards Jewry." *Journal of Jewish Studies* 10 (1959) 97-111.

—. "Relations Between Jews and Christians in the Middle Ages." *Journal of Jewish Studies* 16 (1965) 35-46.

Loeb, Isidore. "Les expulsions des Juifs de France au XIVe siècle." In *Jubelschrift zum siebzigsten Geburtstage des Prof. Dr. H. Graetz*, 1 Abteilung, pp. 39-56. Breslau: S. Schottländer, 1887.

Loenertz, R. "Documents pour servir à l'histoire de la province dominicaine de Grèce (1474-1669)." *Archivum fratrum praedicatorum* 14 (1944) 72-115.

Mack Smith, Denis. *A History of Sicily: Medieval Sicily 800-1713*. London: Chatto and Windus, 1968.

Mansi, Giovanni Domenico. *Sacrorum conciliorum nova et amplissima collectio ... editio novissima*, 31 vols. Florence: 1759-1798.

Marx, Jakob. *Verzeichnis der Handschriften-Sammlung des Hospitals zu Cues*. Trier: Selbst-Verlag des Hospitals, 1905; rpt. Frankfurt: Minerva, 1966.

Maulde la Clavière, René Alphonse Marie de. *Coutumes et règlements de la République d'Avignon au treizième siècle*. Paris: L. Larose, 1879.

—. *Les Juifs dans les états français du Saint-Siège au moyen-âge: documents pour servir à l'histoire des Israélites et de la papauté*. Paris: H. Champion, 1886.

McLaughlin, Terence P., ed. *The Summa Parisiensis on the Decretum Gratiani*. Toronto: Pontifical Institute of Mediaeval Studies, 1952.

Migliorino, Francesco. "Alchimia lecita e illecita nel Trecento: Oldrado da Ponte." *Quaderni medievali* 11 (1981) 6-41.

Mollat, Guillaume. *Jean XXII (1316-1334): Lettres communes*. 16 vols. Paris: Albert Fontemoing, 1904-1947.

Mommsen, Theodor, et al. *Corpus Iuris Civilis*. 3 vols. Berlin: Weidmann, 1892-1895; rpt. Graz: 1967-1970.

Mossé, Armand. *Histoire des Juifs d'Avignon et du Comtat-Venaissin*. Paris: 1934; rpt. Marseille: Laffitte Reprints, 1976.

Muldoon, James. *Popes, Lawyers, and Infidels*. Liverpool: Liverpool University Press, 1979.

Muratori, Lodovico Antonio. *Rerum italicarum scriptores*. 25 vols. in 28. Milan, 1723-1751.

Ogle, Marbury B. "Petrus Comestor, Methodius, and the Saracens." *Speculum* 21 (1946) 318-324.

Pakter, Walter Jay. *De his qui foris sunt: The Teachings of the Medieval Canon and Civil Lawyers concerning the Jews*. Doctoral diss., The Johns Hopkins University, 1974.

Pansier, P. "Les oeuvres de charité juives à Avignon du XIVe au XVIIIe siècle." *Annales d'Avignon* (1924) 71-133.

Panzirolo, G. *De claris legum interpretatibus libri quattuor*. Padua, 1565.

Papias vocabulista [Venice, 1496]; rpt. Turin: Bottega d'Erasmo, 1966.

Powitz, Gerhardt, and Herbert Buck, eds. *Die Handschriften des Bartholomaeusstifts und des Karmeliterklosters in Frankfurt am Main*.

Kataloge der Stadt- und Universitätsbibliothek Frankfurt am Main 3, ed. C. Köttelnesch. Frankfurt: V. Klostermann, 1974.

Prinz, Otto. "Eine frühe abendländische Aktualisierung der lateinischen Übersetzung des Pseudo-Methodius." *Deutsches Archiv für Erforschung des Mittelalters* 41 (1985) 1-23.

Régné, Jean. *History of the Jews in Aragon: Regesta and Documents 1213-1327*. Jerusalem: Magnes Press, Hebrew University, 1978.

Rossi, Vittorio, ed. *Francesco Petrarca: Familiari, edizione critica*. 4 vols. Edizione nazionale delle opere di Francesco Petrarca, 10-13. Florence: G.C. Sansoni, 1968.

Roth, Cecil. "The Feast of Purim and the Blood Accusation." *Speculum* 8 (1933) 520-526.

Riesenberg, Peter. "The Consilia Literature: A Prospectus." *Manuscripta* 6 (1962) 3-22.

Russell, Frederick H. *The Just War in the Middle Ages*. Cambridge: Cambridge University Press, 1975.

Sackur, Ernst. *Sybillinische Texte und Forschungen: Pseudo-Methodius, Adso, und die tiburtinische Sybille*. Halle, 1898; rpt. Turin: Bottega d'Erasmo, 1963.

Sahas, Daniel J. *John of Damascus on Islam*. Leiden: Brill, 1972.

Schneyer, Johann Baptist. *Repertorium der lateinischen Sermones des Mittelalters für die Zeit von 1150-1350*. Beiträge zur Geschichte der Philosophie und Theologie des Mittelalters, ed. M. Schmaus, bd. 43, heft 4. Münster: Aschendorff, 1972.

Schulte, Johann Friedrich von. *Die Geschichte der Quellen und Literatur des canonischen Rechts von Gratian bis auf die Gegenwart*. 3 vols. in 4. Stuttgart: F. Enke, 1875-1880.

Scott, Samuel Parsons, tr. *The Civil Law*. 17 vols. Cincinnati: 1931; rpt. New York: AMS Press, 1973.

Semaan, Khalil I., ed. *Islam and the Medieval West: Aspects of Intercultural Relations*. Albany: State University of New York Press, 1980.

Shatzmiller, Joseph. *Recherches sur la communauté juive de Manosque au moyen-âge 1241–1329*. Paris: Mouton, 1973.

Southern, R.W. *Western Views of Islam in the Middle Ages*. Cambridge, Mass.: Harvard University Press, 1962.

Smalley, Beryl. *The Study of the Bible in the Middle Ages*. Oxford: Blackwell, 1983.

Stalls, William C. "Jewish Conversion to Islam: The Perspective of a *Quaestio*." *Revista Española de Teologia* 43 (1983) 235–251.

Stornajolo, Cosimo, ed. *Codices Urbinates Latini*. Rome: Biblioteca vaticana, 1902.

Stow, Kenneth R. "The Church and the Jews: From St. Paul to Paul IV." In *Bibliographical Essays in Medieval Jewish Studies*, pp. 107–165. The Study of Judaism 2. New York: Anti-Defamation League of B'nai B'rith, 1976.

Synan, Edward A. *The Popes and the Jews in the Middle Ages*. New York: MacMillan, 1965.

Tàutu, Aloysius L. *Acta Honorii III et Gregorii IX*. Pontificia commissio ad redigendum codicem juris canonici orientalis, Fontes, ser. 3, vol. 3. Rome: Biblioteca Vaticana, 1950.

Theiner, August., ed. *Codex diplomaticus dominii temporalis s. sedis*, 3 vols. Rome, 1862; rpt. Frankfurt: Minerva, 1964.

Ullmann, Walter. *Medieval Papalism: The Political Theories of the Medieval Canonists*. London: Methuen, 1949.

Valois, Noel. "Jacques Duèse, pape sous le nom de Jean xxii." *Histoire littéraire de la France* 34 (Paris, 1914) 391-630.

Van Hove, Alphonse. *Prolegomena ad codicem iuris canonici*. Commentarium lovaniense in codicem iuris canonici, 1. 2nd ed. Mechlin: H. Dessain, 1945.

Vidal, J.M. *Benoît XII (1334-1342): Lettres communes analysées d'après les registres dits d'Avignon et du Vatican*. 3 vols. Paris: Albert Fontemoing, 1903-1911.

Watson, Alan, et.al., eds. *The Digest of Justinian*. 4 vols. Philadelphia: University of Pennsylvania Press, 1985.

Watterich, Johann Matthias, ed. *Pontificum Romanorum qui fuerunt inde ab exeunte saeculo IX usque ad finem saeculi XIII vitae ab aequalibus conscriptae, quas ex archivi pontificii, bibliothecae Vaticanae aliarumque codicibus, adiectis suis cuique et annalibus et documentis gravioribus*. 2 vols. Leipzig: W. Engelmann, 1862; rpt. Aalen: Scientia Verlag, 1966.

Will, Eduard. *Die Gutachten des Oldradus de Ponte zum Prozess Heinrichs VII. gegen Robert von Neapel, nebst der Biographie des Oldradus*. Abhandlungen zur mittleren und neueren Geschichte 65. Berlin and Leipzig: W. Rothschild, 1917.

Zacour, Norman. "Papal Regulation of Cardinals' Households in the Fourteenth Century." *Speculum* 50 (1975) 434-455.

Zacour, Norman. "Petrus de Braco and His *Repudium ambitionis*." *Mediaeval Studies* 41 (1979) 1-29.

Index